THIS

Lunch Box Diary

BELONGS TO:

Start Date : _____

End Date : _____

www.sylinalunches.com

Send all inquires to: sylina@sylinalunches.com

Make It Happen Publishing Inc.
ISBN: 978-1-7752476-6-1

DEDICATION

This specially designed book is dedicated to YOU!
Without your dedication to making awesome lunches, there
wouldn't be a need or demand for this type of lunch resource. You
have inspired me to create this Lunch Box Diary
- for inspiring me - I thank you :)

Fill these pages daily with your own lunch ideas, goals, grocery
lists, recipes and thoughts.

- MAKE IT YOUR OWN -

By the time you make it to your last entry, you will have compiled
hundreds of lunch box ideas to launch you into the next year
inspired, well equipped and ready-to-go!

HAPPY LUNCHING

Sylina ♡

YouTube.com/SylinaLunches | Instagram.com/Sylina_Lunches
FaceBook.com/Sylina.Lunches | www.SylinaLunches.com

COMPONENTS OF THIS DIARY
Layout, Guide and Instructions

This diary consists of 20 components:

1. Lunch Packing Tips	11. Sandwiches/Wraps/Rolls
2. Lunch Goals	12. Leftovers for Lunch
3. Lunch Budget	13. Breakfast for Lunch
4. Lunch Staples	14. Removable Grocery List
5. Lunch Shops	15. Recipe Recorder
6. Lunch Inspirations	16. Daily Lunch Box Planner
7. Lunch Books	17. Weekly Lunch Box Planner
8. Seasonal Produce	18. Year in Lunches Log
9. Ideas for Produce	19. Year Overview Calendar
10. Protein Options	20. Lunch Notes & Jokes

How to use this diary:

You will find that each section is designed so that you can easily know how to utilize the pages. It's really as simple as filling out a questionnaire. To make it even more clear, here are some explanations!

Step One: The first thing you should do is clearly state your lunch goals and lunch budget on page 10 and 11.

Step Two: Go to page 20 to 26 and look over all the fruits, vegetables and protein options, record which ones you like, don't like, unsure about, and which you have never tried before - use the column on the left side. At the end of the year, go back and do this again using the column on the right. Did anything change? Did you find that you branched out and tried more foods?

Step Three: Everything else can be filled out as you go along. When you find yourself eating the same things over and over - add it to your *Lunch Staples* page. Find a store you love, add it to your *Lunch Shops* page etc. - **NOW GET PLANNING!**

See the images on the next page for instructions regarding your actual lunch planning pages.

DAILY LUNCH PLANNER

Mark down the date

What did you drink today? Water, juice, smoothie or something else? (record how many you had)

Record any recipes or notes about your lunch

Think ahead and reflect on the day's lunch

Some food for thought and inspiring food quotes

Removable Grocery List

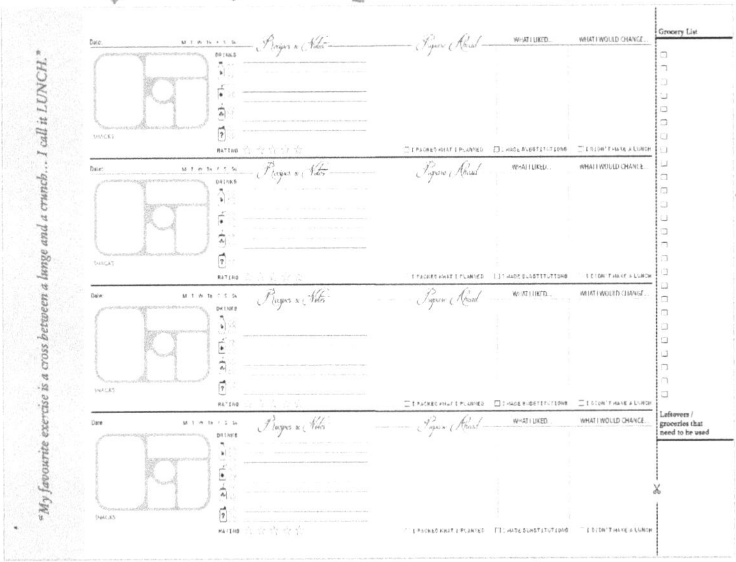

Try to use up these items first when you're planning your lunches

Plan out your daily lunches and snacks using the Bengto Kids template

"My favourite exercise is a cross between a lunge and a crunch... I call it LUNCH."
Date:
DRINKS
Recipes & Notes
Prepare Ahead
WHAT I LIKED...
WHAT I WOULD CHANGE...
SNACKS
RATING
Grocery List
Leftovers / groceries that need to be used

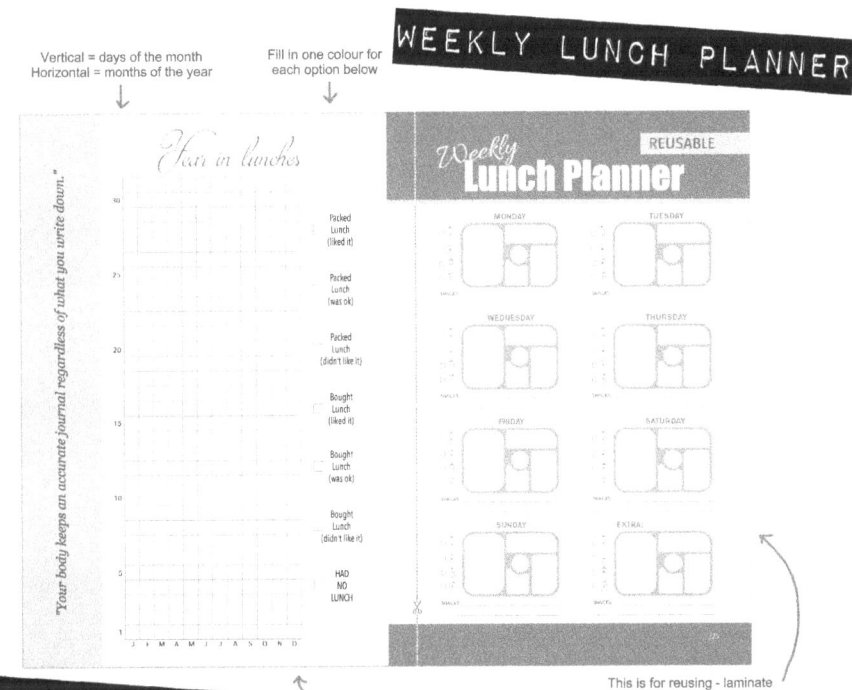

Did you enjoy your lunch? Give it a rating so you can easily see which ones were a hit.

Sometimes what you plan isn't what you pack - keeping a record will help you stay accountable

WEEKLY LUNCH PLANNER

Vertical = days of the month
Horizontal = months of the year

Fill in one colour for each option below

"Your body keeps an accurate journal regardless of what you write down."
Year in lunches
Packed Lunch (liked it)
Packed Lunch (was ok)
Packed Lunch (didn't like it)
Bought Lunch (liked it)
Bought Lunch (was ok)
Bought Lunch (didn't like it)
HAD NO LUNCH
J F M A M J J A S O N D

REUSABLE
Weekly Lunch Planner
MONDAY
TUESDAY
WEDNESDAY
THURSDAY
FRIDAY
SATURDAY
SUNDAY
EXTRA:

YEAR OVERVIEW

Add the colour to the graph for every day of the year

This is for reusing - laminate it or put it into a page protector so that you can erase and reuse it every week.

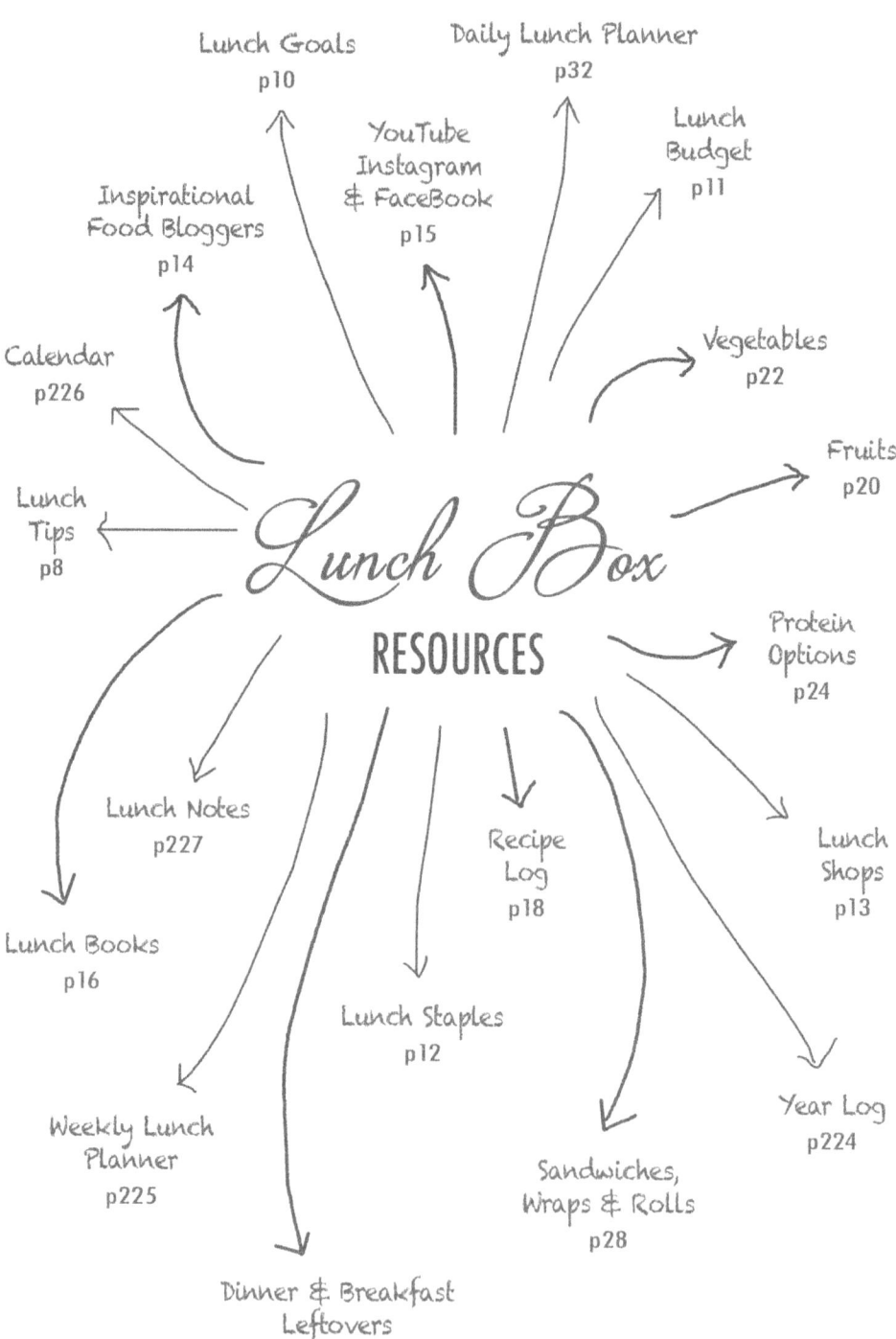

Lunch Goals
p10

Daily Lunch Planner
p32

YouTube
Instagram
& FaceBook
p15

Lunch
Budget
p11

Inspirational
Food Bloggers
p14

Calendar
p226

Vegetables
p22

Fruits
p20

Lunch
Tips
p8

Lunch Box

RESOURCES

Protein
Options
p24

Lunch Notes
p227

Recipe
Log
p18

Lunch
Shops
p13

Lunch Books
p16

Lunch Staples
p12

Year Log
p224

Weekly Lunch
Planner
p225

Sandwiches,
Wraps & Rolls
p28

Dinner & Breakfast
Leftovers
p30

TABLE OF CONTENTS

*Add the titles and page numbers for any personalized content that was added to your diary. Extra blank pages have been included to the end of this book.

20 Tips
for packing *Lunches*

Here are some ways to stay organized, motivated and inspired to make and enjoy your lunches...

1 SET LUNCH GOALS

What is it you want from packing lunches? Do you want to eat healthier, save money, save time etc. Just knowing what it is you are expecting can help you to stay motivated!

2 SET A LUNCH BUDGET

Setting a budget for lunch can help you to stay on track. Not only will you be more inclined to pack lunch instead of buying it - you'll be forced to be more creative with using leftovers and homemade foods rather than packaged snacks.

3 HAVE THE RIGHT STUFF

Yes, having a good quality lunch box is important but you also need to have the right tools too. What those tools are, depends on what you like. Want cute lunches? Get some cute food picks or silicone liners. Want more textures in your food? Get a julienne peeler or crinkle cutter. Having the right stuff also applies to food - so don't forget to also stock up your pantry & fridge.

4 CREATE GOOD HABITS

Having a routine will make the whole lunch making process easier. Designate a place for your lunch supplies and an area in the fridge for your lunch foods. Whether you pack your lunches right after dinner or first thing in the morning - pick a time and stick to it. Just as important as making your lunch, you should also get into the habit of cleaning up afterwards too!

5 PLAN IN ADVANCE

Pre-plan which days you plan on buying or making lunch. Seeing it planned out can help you visualize what is needed for the week. Now prep any fruits, veggies or grains that you'll need. This will save you time!

6 BALANCE IS KEY

Simply put, get into the habit of packing a variety of different foods and make a conscious effort to include a little bit from each food group.

7 MAKE IT TASTE GOOD!

If you don't like it, you probably won't eat it! It's ok to try new foods - just pack smaller portions of it BUT be sure to actually pack foods that you enjoy eating. Fill your lunch with yummy flavors!

8 MAKE IT *Pretty*!

We eat with our eyes - so make it look appetizing by including lots of colors, textures and shapes. You'll be surprised to find that a few "pretty" items can make all the difference in what you eat as well as how much of it you eat.

9 EAT WHAT'S IN SEASON

Not only will your fruits & veggies taste better when they're in season, you'll also end up spending less! Don't forget - what grows together, goes together - so if you're buying in season, it'll be easy to whip up a meal that tastes great.

10 USE YOUR LEFTOVERS

Leftovers are your friends! Use them as is or reinvent them into something new by simply adding some fresh ingredients or presenting them in a new way. You'll find that eventually you'll start making extra dinner just for lunches! You could even portion them out into individual servings and freeze them for emergency lunches.

11 HAVE LUNCH STAPLES

Are there certain foods you enjoy having for lunch? Make a list of what you find yourself using the most and always have them stocked. Utilize your pantry, fridge and freezer. You'll be surprised how many of your favorite foods freeze well.

12 HAVE SNACKS AVAILABLE

Keep a variety of snacks available. If there are some packaged snacks you like, keep them stocked in your pantry. Also batch baking cookies, muffins, biscuits etc. and freezing them will make it easy to just grab one out either the night before or in the morning.

13 BE FLEXIBLE

Things don't always go as planned so be flexible and adjust accordingly. It's ok to not follow what you had planned - go with the flow. It won't be the end of the world if you ran out of tortillas and can't make that wrap you had planned - turn it into a salad instead or be creative and come up with something different to wrap it with!

14 COLLECT SAUCE PACKETS

No matter how much you love cooking at home, we all find ourselves eating out or ordering in at some point. When you do - be sure to keep and collect any sauce packets - these will come in handy for your packed lunches! Ketchup, mustard, soy sauce, dressing or even just salt and pepper.

15 BE MINDFUL

Be mindful about what you are packing and how you feel after eating the food you pack for lunch. Was it enough food? Did it give you the energy you needed for the day? Also be mindful about how you pack your lunch to avoid soggy messes or mixing of foods that don't go well together.

16 KEEP IDEAS & RECIPES

When you come across a lunch idea or recipe that you really enjoyed - be sure to record it for future reference. Having these readily available will become like a personal lunch menu!

17 FOOD SAFETY

Keep your food safe by using an ice pack and an insulated lunch bag to avoid food spoilage. This will also help to keep your fruits and veggies looking fresh. During the hotter months, things like drinks, yogurts, baked goods etc. can be packed frozen into your lunch and they'll help keep things cold and be thawed and ready by lunch time.

18 ALWAYS PACK A TREAT

Everyone looks forward to having a treat! Be it something sweet or something savoury, give yourself a little something to look forward to and enjoy at lunch time. Packing it in your lunch will help to avoid those mid afternoon cravings!

19 ALWAYS PACK WATER

We all know staying hydrated is important - so don't forget to pack some water. Don't like water? Make it more interesting by adding some frozen fruit to it! If you pack it, you'll be more likely to drink it!

20 TAKE IT EASY!

Give yourself a break - it's ok if you skip a day! Cheat days, days off or even "I'm too busy" or "I'm feeling lazy" days are totally OK!

MY *Lunch* GOALS

MAIN LUNCH GOAL:

I will pack my lunch...

☐ in the morning   ☐ after dinner   ☐ in the evening   ☐ at _____ o'clock

I will clean my lunch box...

☐ when I get home   ☐ after dinner   ☐ in the evening   ☐ at _____ o'clock

☐ _____

☐ _____

☐ _____

☐ _____

☐ _____

☐ _____

☐ _____

☐ _____

☐ _____

SOME IDEAS:
☐ Spend less on lunch   ☐ Drink more water
☐ Eat more vegetables   ☐ Eat more whole foods
☐ Pack lunches more often   ☐ Enjoy my lunch
☐ Meal prep snacks   ☐ Waste less food

MY *Lunch* BUDGET $

SUPPLIES

Lunch Box $ _____
Lunch Bag $ _____
Water Bottle $ _____
Ice Pack $ _____

_____
_____
_____
_____
_____
_____
_____
_____
_____
_____
_____
_____
_____
_____
_____
_____
_____
_____

TOTAL $ _____

MONTHLY FOOD ALLOWANCE

MONTH: _____

	BUDGET	SPENT
Produce	$	$
Snacks	$	$
Drinks	$	$
Eating Out	$	$
Other Stuff	$	$
TOTAL	$	$

MONTH: _____

	BUDGET	SPENT
Produce	$	$
Snacks	$	$
Drinks	$	$
Eating Out	$	$
Other Stuff	$	$
TOTAL	$	$

MONTH: _____

	BUDGET	SPENT
Produce	$	$
Snacks	$	$
Drinks	$	$
Eating Out	$	$
Other Stuff	$	$
TOTAL	$	$

MONTH: _____

	BUDGET	SPENT
Produce	$	$
Snacks	$	$
Drinks	$	$
Eating Out	$	$
Other Stuff	$	$
TOTAL	$	$

MONTH: _____

	BUDGET	SPENT
Produce	$	$
Snacks	$	$
Drinks	$	$
Eating Out	$	$
Other Stuff	$	$
TOTAL	$	$

MONTH: _____

	BUDGET	SPENT
Produce	$	$
Snacks	$	$
Drinks	$	$
Eating Out	$	$
Other Stuff	$	$
TOTAL	$	$

MONTH: _____

	BUDGET	SPENT
Produce	$	$
Snacks	$	$
Drinks	$	$
Eating Out	$	$
Other Stuff	$	$
TOTAL	$	$

MONTH: _____

	BUDGET	SPENT
Produce	$	$
Snacks	$	$
Drinks	$	$
Eating Out	$	$
Other Stuff	$	$
TOTAL	$	$

MONTH: _____

	BUDGET	SPENT
Produce	$	$
Snacks	$	$
Drinks	$	$
Eating Out	$	$
Other Stuff	$	$
TOTAL	$	$

EXCEPTIONS & UNEXPECTED EXPENSES:

☐ _____   ☐ _____   ☐ _____
☐ _____   ☐ _____   ☐ _____
☐ _____   ☐ _____   ☐ _____

My *Lunch* STAPLES

FRIDGE

- ☐ _____
- ☐ _____
- ☐ _____
- ☐ _____
- ☐ _____
- ☐ _____
- ☐ _____
- ☐ _____
- ☐ _____
- ☐ _____
- ☐ _____
- ☐ _____
- ☐ _____
- ☐ _____
- ☐ _____
- ☐ _____
- ☐ _____
- ☐ _____
- ☐ _____
- ☐ _____
- ☐ _____
- ☐ _____
- ☐ _____

FREEZER

- ☐ _____
- ☐ _____
- ☐ _____
- ☐ _____
- ☐ _____
- ☐ _____
- ☐ _____
- ☐ _____
- ☐ _____
- ☐ _____
- ☐ _____
- ☐ _____
- ☐ _____
- ☐ _____
- ☐ _____
- ☐ _____
- ☐ _____
- ☐ _____
- ☐ _____
- ☐ _____
- ☐ _____
- ☐ _____
- ☐ _____

PANTRY

- ☐ _____
- ☐ _____
- ☐ _____
- ☐ _____
- ☐ _____
- ☐ _____
- ☐ _____
- ☐ _____
- ☐ _____
- ☐ _____
- ☐ _____
- ☐ _____
- ☐ _____
- ☐ _____
- ☐ _____
- ☐ _____
- ☐ _____
- ☐ _____
- ☐ _____
- ☐ _____
- ☐ _____
- ☐ _____
- ☐ _____

NON FOOD STAPLES:

- ☐ _____
- ☐ _____
- ☐ _____
- ☐ _____
- ☐ _____
- ☐ _____
- ☐ _____
- ☐ _____
- ☐ _____

My list of *Lunch* SHOPS

FOR SUPPLIES

- [ ]
- [ ]
- [ ]
- [ ]
- [ ]
- [ ]
- [ ]
- [ ]
- [ ]
- [ ]
- [ ]
- [ ]
- [ ]
- [ ]
- [ ]
- [ ]
- [ ]
- [ ]
- [ ]
- [ ]
- [ ]
- [ ]

FOR FOOD

- [ ]
- [ ]
- [ ]
- [ ]
- [ ]
- [ ]
- [ ]
- [ ]
- [ ]
- [ ]
- [ ]
- [ ]
- [ ]
- [ ]
- [ ]
- [ ]
- [ ]
- [ ]
- [ ]
- [ ]
- [ ]
- [ ]

SOME RECOMMENDATIONS:

Lunch Stuff:
www.amazon.com
www.bentousa.com
www.cutekidstuff.com
www.sayplease.com

Food & Snacks:
www.costco.com
www.thrivemarket.com
www.walmart.com
www.wholefoods.com

Lunch Apps:
www.lalalunchbox.com
www.mealime.com
www.todaysparent.com (mealtime)
www.yummly.com

RESOURCES FOR LUNCH IDEAS

Places to go to find amazing lunch ideas & recipes.

Food Blogs:
Here are some of my favorite blogs.

Add to the list with your favorites!

www.100daysofrealfood.com
www.annabelkarmel.com
www.babyfoode.com
www.becomingabentoholic.com
www.bentgo.com
www.bentomonsters.com
www.bentoschoollunches.com
www.casey2cook.com
www.cookieandkate.com
www.easytoddlermeals.com
www.eatsamazing.co.uk
www.fablunch.com
www.familyfreshmeals.com
www.greenkitchenstories.com
www.iamafoodblog.com
www.kidgredients.com.au
www.lalalunchbox.com
www.laurafuentes.com
www.littlemissbento.com
www.mamabelly.com
www.momskitchenhandbook.com
www.onehungrymama.com
www.produceforkids.com
www.superhealthykids.com
www.sweetpotatochronicles.com
www.the-fit-foodie.com
www.thekitchn.com
www.weelicious.com
www.wendolonia.com
www.whatlisacooks.com
www.wholefully.com

FaceBook: The best thing about joining a FaceBook lunch group is that you'll find other people who are happy to share and swap recipes that they use for lunches, ask questions, get answers and contribute to lunch related discussions. Joining a local lunch group or one specific to your dietary needs can also help make finding lunch supplies or recipes easier.

Join my private FaceBook Bento Lunch Groups here:
Canada: www.facebook.com/groups/bentolunchboxideascanada
USA: www.facebook.com/groups/bentolunchboxideasusa

YouTube: Definitely check out these channels for delicious lunch and snack recipes.

www.youtube.com/bellabooslunches
www.youtube.com/caitlinshoemaker
www.youtube.com/danispies
www.youtube.com/fablunch
www.youtube.com/gemmastafford
www.youtube.com/honeysucklecatering
www.youtube.com/hotforfood
www.youtube.com/laurainthekitchen
www.youtube.com/marystestkitchen
www.youtube.com/mindovermunch
www.youtube.com/momables
www.youtube.com/ochikeron
www.youtube.com/onehungrymama
www.youtube.com/pickuplimes
www.youtube.com/sylinalunches
www.youtube.com/tastyjunior
www.youtube.com/thedomesticgeek1
www.youtube.com/thrivingonplants
www.youtube.com/weelicious

INSTAGRAM & PINTEREST

Search using tags like:

#bento
#bentoart
#bentobox
#bentgo
#bentgolunch
#foodforkids
#kidslunch
#kidslunchbox
#lunchbox
#lunchboxes
#lunchboxideas
#lunches
#lunchgoals
#lunchideas
#lunchprep
#mealprep
#packedlunch
#schoollunch
#schoollunchideas
#snacks
#snackideas
#worklunch

Find my lunch ideas here:

@Sylina_Lunches

Sylina Lunches

Little Bento *by Michele Olivier*

Best Lunch Box Ever: *Ideas and Recipes for School Lunches Kids Will Love* by Katie Sullivan Morford

EVERYDAY BENTO: *50 Cute and Yummy Lunches To Go* by Wendy Thorpe Copley

The Just Bento Cookbook: Everyday Lunches To Go by Makiko Itoh

LAURA IN THE **KITCHEN** by Laura Vitale

Effortless Bento: 300 Japanese Box Lunch Recipes by Shufuno-Tomo

MIX + MATCH LUNCHBOX: *Over 27,000 Wholesome Combos to Make Lunch Go Yum!* by Cherie Schetselaar

GREEN KITCHEN AT HOME by David Frenkiel and Luise Vindahl

WEELICIOUS LUNCHES *Think outside the Lunch Box with More Than 160 Happier Meals* by Catherine McCord

THE BEST HOMEMADE KIDS' LUNCHES ON THE PLANET by Laura Fuentes

The School Year Survival Cookbook *Laura Keogh & Ceri Marsh*

BEATING THE **LUNCH BOX BLUES** by J. M. HIRSCH

BIG BENTO BOOK *by Alyssia Sheikh*

Yum-Yum Bento Box: *Fresh Recipes for Adorable Lunches* by Maki Ogawa

MAKE IT *Easy:* *120 Mix-and-Match Recipes to Cook from Scratch* by Stacie Billis

MY FAVORITE RECIPES

Recipe *Index*

AUTHOR	BOOK OR SOURCE

When you find something you love...
Record it here so it's easy to find your favorite lunch recipes!

RECIPE NAME	MAIN	SIDE	SNACK	TREAT	DRINK	PAGE
	○	○	○	○	○	
	○	○	○	○	○	
	○	○	○	○	○	
	○	○	○	○	○	
	○	○	○	○	○	
	○	○	○	○	○	
	○	○	○	○	○	
	○	○	○	○	○	
	○	○	○	○	○	
	○	○	○	○	○	
	○	○	○	○	○	
	○	○	○	○	○	
	○	○	○	○	○	
	○	○	○	○	○	
	○	○	○	○	○	
	○	○	○	○	○	
	○	○	○	○	○	
	○	○	○	○	○	
	○	○	○	○	○	
	○	○	○	○	○	
	○	○	○	○	○	
	○	○	○	○	○	
	○	○	○	○	○	
	○	○	○	○	○	
	○	○	○	○	○	
	○	○	○	○	○	
	○	○	○	○	○	
	○	○	○	○	○	
	○	○	○	○	○	
	○	○	○	○	○	
	○	○	○	○	○	
	○	○	○	○	○	
	○	○	○	○	○	

Seasonal Fruits

	?	:)	:|	:(	WINTER	SPRING	SUMMER	FALL	?	:)	:|	:(
Acai Berries	○	○	○	○	Available all year frozen or in powder form - near impossible to get fresh				○	○	○	○
Apples	○	○	○	○					○	○	○	○
Apricots	○	○	○	○					○	○	○	○
*Avocados	○	○	○	○	Typically available year round from tropical regions				○	○	○	○
Bananas	○	○	○	○	There's no excuse - eat them year round - they're usually pretty cheap!				○	○	○	○
Blackberries	○	○	○	○					○	○	○	○
Blueberries	○	○	○	○					○	○	○	○
Cantaloupes	○	○	○	○					○	○	○	○
Cherries	○	○	○	○					○	○	○	○
Clementines	○	○	○	○					○	○	○	○
Coconuts	○	○	○	○	Typically available year round from tropical regions				○	○	○	○
Cranberries	○	○	○	○					○	○	○	○
*Cucumbers	○	○	○	○					○	○	○	○
Currants	○	○	○	○					○	○	○	○
Dates	○	○	○	○					○	○	○	○
Dragonfruits	○	○	○	○	Peak season is in the summer/fall but available year round from tropical regions				○	○	○	○
Durian	○	○	○	○					○	○	○	○
Figs	○	○	○	○					○	○	○	○
Goji Berries	○	○	○	○	Available all year in dehydrated form				○	○	○	○
Gooseberries	○	○	○	○					○	○	○	○
Grapefruits	○	○	○	○					○	○	○	○
Grapes	○	○	○	○					○	○	○	○
Guava	○	○	○	○					○	○	○	○
Honeydew Melon	○	○	○	○					○	○	○	○
Jackfruit	○	○	○	○					○	○	○	○
Kiwi	○	○	○	○					○	○	○	○
Kumquats	○	○	○	○					○	○	○	○
Longan	○	○	○	○					○	○	○	○
Lychee	○	○	○	○					○	○	○	○
Mandarines	○	○	○	○					○	○	○	○
Mangoes	○	○	○	○					○	○	○	○
Mangosteens	○	○	○	○					○	○	○	○
Mulberries	○	○	○	○					○	○	○	○
Nectarines	○	○	○	○					○	○	○	○
*Olives	○	○	○	○	Available all year preserved and jarred				○	○	○	○
Oranges	○	○	○	○					○	○	○	○
Papaya	○	○	○	○					○	○	○	○
Passion Fruit	○	○	○	○					○	○	○	○
Peaches	○	○	○	○					○	○	○	○
Pears	○	○	○	○					○	○	○	○
Persimmons	○	○	○	○					○	○	○	○
Pineapples	○	○	○	○					○	○	○	○
Plantains	○	○	○	○	Typically available year round from tropical regions				○	○	○	○
Plums	○	○	○	○					○	○	○	○
Pomegranates	○	○	○	○					○	○	○	○
Prunes	○	○	○	○	Because it is a dried plum - it's available year round				○	○	○	○
Quince	○	○	○	○					○	○	○	○
Raisins	○	○	○	○	Because it is a dried grape - it's available year round				○	○	○	○
Raspberries	○	○	○	○					○	○	○	○
**Rhubarb	○	○	○	○					○	○	○	○
Starfruit	○	○	○	○					○	○	○	○
Strawberries	○	○	○	○					○	○	○	○
Tangerines	○	○	○	○					○	○	○	○
*Tomatoes	○	○	○	○					○	○	○	○
Watermelon	○	○	○	○					○	○	○	○

*BECAUSE OF THEIR USE IN SAVORY RECIPES, MANY WOULD CONSIDER THESE AS VEGETABLES BUT THEY ARE IN FACT FRUITS!
**THIS IS ACTUALLY A VEGETABLE BUT MANY PEOPLE USE IT AS A FRUIT IN DESSERTS AND OTHER SWEET RECIPES.

WAYS TO PACK YOUR ...**FRUITS** FOR LUNCH

Just the way they are!

Bake them into muffins

Make some kabobs

Create fun shapes like apple cars

Puréed into jam or sauce

Make some mini pies or tarts

Turn them into fruit leather!

Apple or Banana Sandwiches

Make some wraps with fruit and cream cheese or nut butters

Topped over yogurt, pudding or in a yogurt parfait

Blend them into smoothies

Mix with gelatin or agar agar to make fruit gummies

Dipped in chocolate

Tossed into a fruit salad

Dehydrated

Seasonal Vegetables

	?	⚥	⚥	⚥	WINTER	SPRING	SUMMER	FALL	?	⚥	⚥	⚥
Artichoke	○	○	○	○					○	○	○	○
Arugula	○	○	○	○					○	○	○	○
Asparagus	○	○	○	○					○	○	○	○
Bamboo Shoots	○	○	○	○					○	○	○	○
Beets	○	○	○	○					○	○	○	○
Bok Choy	○	○	○	○					○	○	○	○
Broccoli	○	○	○	○					○	○	○	○
Broccolini	○	○	○	○					○	○	○	○
Brussel Sprouts	○	○	○	○					○	○	○	○
Cabbage	○	○	○	○	Always in season!				○	○	○	○
Capers	○	○	○	○	Typically in a preserved form - they are available year round				○	○	○	○
Carrots	○	○	○	○					○	○	○	○
Cauliflower	○	○	○	○					○	○	○	○
Celery	○	○	○	○					○	○	○	○
Collard Greens	○	○	○	○					○	○	○	○
Corn	○	○	○	○					○	○	○	○
*Cucumbers	○	○	○	○					○	○	○	○
Daikon	○	○	○	○					○	○	○	○
Dandelion Greens	○	○	○	○					○	○	○	○
Edamame	○	○	○	○					○	○	○	○
Eggplant	○	○	○	○					○	○	○	○
Endives	○	○	○	○					○	○	○	○
Fiddleheads	○	○	○	○					○	○	○	○
Green Beans	○	○	○	○					○	○	○	○
Hearts of Palm	○	○	○	○	Typically available from tropical regions and jarred				○	○	○	○
Jicama	○	○	○	○					○	○	○	○
Kale	○	○	○	○					○	○	○	○
Lettuce	○	○	○	○					○	○	○	○
Lotus Root	○	○	○	○					○	○	○	○
Mushrooms	○	○	○	○					○	○	○	○
Okra	○	○	○	○					○	○	○	○
Parsnips	○	○	○	○					○	○	○	○
Peas	○	○	○	○					○	○	○	○
Peppers	○	○	○	○					○	○	○	○
Potatoes	○	○	○	○					○	○	○	○
Pumpkin	○	○	○	○					○	○	○	○
Radicchio	○	○	○	○					○	○	○	○
Radishes	○	○	○	○					○	○	○	○
Rapini	○	○	○	○					○	○	○	○
Rutabagas	○	○	○	○					○	○	○	○
Snow Peas	○	○	○	○					○	○	○	○
Snow Pea Leaves	○	○	○	○					○	○	○	○
Spinach	○	○	○	○	Available year round				○	○	○	○
Squash	○	○	○	○					○	○	○	○
Sugar Snap Peas	○	○	○	○					○	○	○	○
Sweet Potatoes	○	○	○	○					○	○	○	○
Swiss Chard	○	○	○	○					○	○	○	○
*Tamatillo	○	○	○	○					○	○	○	○
Taro	○	○	○	○					○	○	○	○
*Tomatoes	○	○	○	○					○	○	○	○
Turnips	○	○	○	○					○	○	○	○
Water Chestnut	○	○	○	○	Typically available from semi-tropical regions - usually canned				○	○	○	○
Watercress	○	○	○	○					○	○	○	○
Yams	○	○	○	○					○	○	○	○
Zucchini	○	○	○	○					○	○	○	○

*BECAUSE OF THEIR USE IN SAVORY RECIPES, MANY WOULD CONSIDER THESE AS VEGETABLES BUT THEY ARE IN FACT FRUITS!

**THERE MAY BE SLIGHT REGIONAL AND SEASONAL DIFFERENCES DEPENDING ON WHERE YOU LIVE. THIS IS A GENERAL GUIDE.

Things to make with ... **VEGETABLES**

Turn them into nuggets

The easiest and fastest way to to eat them - just the way they are!

Put them on a pizza

Bake them into muffins

Blend them into a smoothie or green juice

Put it on a kabob

Add them to pasta as sauce or whole

Spiralize them into noodles

Make some VEGGIE chips!

Chop them into a quiche

Put it in a roll

Cook it in some soup

Add them in a sandwich

Make a salad!

Soup

Put them in some sushi

Protein Options

	?	:)	:|	:(	PORTION	CALORIES	PROTEIN	?	:)	:|	:(
Beef	○	○	○	○	100g	288	26.33g	○	○	○	○
- Beef Jerky	○	○	○	○	1 Large Piece	82	6.64g	○	○	○	○
- Brisket	○	○	○	○	1 Thin Slice	72	5.22g	○	○	○	○
- Corned Beef	○	○	○	○	Per Slice	53	3.82g	○	○	○	○
- Ground Beef	○	○	○	○	1 Small Meatball	39	3.55g	○	○	○	○
- Roast Beef	○	○	○	○	Per Slice	56	5.44g	○	○	○	○
- Steak	○	○	○	○	1 Small Steak	386	41.75g	○	○	○	○
Bison	○	○	○	○	1 Medium Patty	122	24.17g	○	○	○	○
Buffalo	○	○	○	○	100g	99	20.39g	○	○	○	○
Cheese	○	○	○	○	1 Slice	84	5.33g	○	○	○	○
Chicken	○	○	○	○	100g	237	30.42g	○	○	○	○
- Breasts	○	○	○	○	1 Thin Slice	14	2.07g	○	○	○	○
- Thighs	○	○	○	○	1 Small Thigh	135	13.67g	○	○	○	○
- Wings	○	○	○	○	1 Small Wing	81	7.46g	○	○	○	○
- Ground Chicken	○	○	○	○	1 Small Patty	114	12.99g	○	○	○	○
- Drumsticks	○	○	○	○	1 Small Drumstick	81	10.18g	○	○	○	○
Duck	○	○	○	○	1/2 Breast	255	14.37g	○	○	○	○
Eggs	○	○	○	○	1 Large Boiled Egg	77	6.26g	○	○	○	○
Fish	○	○	○	○	100g	112	23.3g	○	○	○	○
- Anchovies	○	○	○	○	1 Anchovy	8	1.16g	○	○	○	○
- Cod	○	○	○	○	1 Fillet	196	17.86g	○	○	○	○
- Halibut	○	○	○	○	1/2 Fillet	224	42.45g	○	○	○	○
- Herring	○	○	○	○	100g	158	17.96g	○	○	○	○
- Mackerel	○	○	○	○	100g	222	22.56g	○	○	○	○
- Mahi Mahi	○	○	○	○	1 Fillet	100	21.76g	○	○	○	○
- Perch	○	○	○	○	1 Fillet	69	11.09g	○	○	○	○
- Pollock	○	○	○	○	1 Fillet	104	23g	○	○	○	○
- Rainbow Trout	○	○	○	○	1 Fillet	118	15.35g	○	○	○	○
- Salmon	○	○	○	○	1 Fillet	472	66.16g	○	○	○	○
- Sardines	○	○	○	○	1 Small Sardine	10	1.23g	○	○	○	○
- Sea Bass	○	○	○	○	1 Fillet	152	22.82g	○	○	○	○
- Tilapia	○	○	○	○	1 Fillet	100	20g	○	○	○	○
- Tuna	○	○	○	○	1 Can	194	42.6g	○	○	○	○
Greek Yogurt	○	○	○	○	1/2 Cup	110	4.5g	○	○	○	○
Kefir	○	○	○	○	1/2 Cup	67	3.7g	○	○	○	○
Lamb	○	○	○	○	100g	292	24.32g	○	○	○	○
Pork	○	○	○	○	100g	271	27.34g	○	○	○	○
- Bacon	○	○	○	○	1 Thin Slice	27	1.85g	○	○	○	○
- Chops	○	○	○	○	1 Thin Chop	118	13.12g	○	○	○	○
- Ham	○	○	○	○	Per Slice	46	4.65g	○	○	○	○
- Ground Pork	○	○	○	○	100g	263	16.88g	○	○	○	○
- Tenderloin	○	○	○	○	100g	185	31.65g	○	○	○	○
Seafood	○	○	○	○	52oz Seafood Medley	80	16g	○	○	○	○
- Clams	○	○	○	○	1 Small Clam	7	1.15g	○	○	○	○
- Crab	○	○	○	○	100g	101	20.03g	○	○	○	○
- Lobster	○	○	○	○	100g	97	20.33g	○	○	○	○
- Mussels	○	○	○	○	1 Small Mussel	7	0.69g	○	○	○	○
- Octopus	○	○	○	○	100g	188	16.94g	○	○	○	○
- Oysters	○	○	○	○	1 Oyster	13	0.73g	○	○	○	○
- Scallops	○	○	○	○	1 Scallop	35	2.9g	○	○	○	○
- Shrimp	○	○	○	○	1 Shrimp	7	1.38g	○	○	○	○
Turkey	○	○	○	○	Per Slice	119	21.77g	○	○	○	○
- Turkey Breasts	○	○	○	○	100g	50	9g	○	○	○	○
- Ground Turkey	○	○	○	○	1 Small Patty	112	13.02g	○	○	○	○
Whey Protein	○	○	○	○	1 Scoop	120	25g	○	○	○	○

*ALL NUMBERS WILL VARY DEPENDING ON YOUR COOKING METHOD. THESE APPROXIMATIONS APPLY TO COOKED PROTEINS.

**THE RECOMMENDED DIETARY ALLOWANCE FOR PROTEIN IS 0.8 GRAMS OF PROTEIN PER KILOGRAM OF BODY WEIGHT.

Favorite Protein Recipes and Ideas:

When you've discovered an awesome product, recipe or idea to incorporate more protein into your meals - be sure to jot them down here for future reference!

**PROTEIN IDEAS
to get you started:**

- Baked Protein
- Bite Sized Pieces
- Boiled Protein
- Burgers
- Burritos
- Calzones
- Chia Puddings
- Custards
- Cutlets
- Empanadas
- Enchiladas
- Falafels
- Fried Rice
- Fritters
- Gazpacho
- Granola
- Grilled Protein
- Hot Dogs
- Jerky
- Kabobs
- Kimchi
- Lasagna
- Lunchables
- Meat Balls
- Muffin Cups
- Nuggets
-Overnight Oats
- Parfaits
- Pastas
- Pickled Protein
- Pies/Tarts
- Pitas
- Pizzas
- Porridge
- Protein Balls

Plant Based *Protein Options*

	?	⏝	⏝	⏝	PORTION	CALORIES	PROTEIN	?	⏝	⏝	⏝
Artichokes	○	○	○	○	1 Small Globe	69	3.47g	○	○	○	○
Asparagus	○	○	○	○	1 Small Spear	5	0.28g	○	○	○	○
Avocado	○	○	○	○	1 Avocado	322	4.02g	○	○	○	○
Beans	○	○	○	○	100g	115	7.09g	○	○	○	○
Broccoli	○	○	○	○	1 Stalk	51	4.26g	○	○	○	○
Brown Rice	○	○	○	○	100g	110	2.56g	○	○	○	○
Brussels Sprouts	○	○	○	○	1 Sprout	8	0.53g	○	○	○	○
Buckwheat	○	○	○	○	100g	92	3.38g	○	○	○	○
Cabbage	○	○	○	○	1 Small Leaf	6	0.14g	○	○	○	○
Cauliflower	○	○	○	○	1 Floweret	5	0.39g	○	○	○	○
Chia Seeds	○	○	○	○	1 Tablespoon	60	3g	○	○	○	○
Chickpeas	○	○	○	○	100g	119	4.95g	○	○	○	○
Chlorella	○	○	○	○	1 Tablespoon	20	4g	○	○	○	○
Couscous	○	○	○	○	100g	112	3.79g	○	○	○	○
Cucumbers	○	○	○	○	1 Whole Cucumber	45	1.96g	○	○	○	○
Edamame	○	○	○	○	1/2 Cup	120	13g	○	○	○	○
Ezekiel Bread	○	○	○	○	1 Slice	80	4g	○	○	○	○
Figs	○	○	○	○	1 Small Fig	30	0.3g	○	○	○	○
Flaxseeds	○	○	○	○	1 Tablespoon	37	1.28g	○	○	○	○
Goji Berries	○	○	○	○	1/4 Cup	100	4g	○	○	○	○
Greek Yogurt	○	○	○	○	1/2 Cup	110	4.5g	○	○	○	○
Green Beans	○	○	○	○	1 Green Bean	2	0.10g	○	○	○	○
Hearts of Palm	○	○	○	○	1 Piece	9	0.83g	○	○	○	○
Hemp Protein	○	○	○	○	1 Tablespoon	55	7.5g	○	○	○	○
Hummus	○	○	○	○	1 Tablespoon	27	0.73g	○	○	○	○
Kale	○	○	○	○	100g	50	3.3g	○	○	○	○
Leafy Greens	○	○	○	○	100g	45	1.69g	○	○	○	○
Lentils	○	○	○	○	100g	165	8.39g	○	○	○	○
Maca Powder	○	○	○	○	1 Tablespoon	50	2g	○	○	○	○
Nut Butters	○	○	○	○	1 Tablespoon	100	3.5g	○	○	○	○
Nut Milks	○	○	○	○	1 Cup	30	1g	○	○	○	○
Nuts	○	○	○	○	1/4 Cup	200	5g	○	○	○	○
Oats	○	○	○	○	100g	389	16.89g	○	○	○	○
Oatmeal	○	○	○	○	100g	62	2.59g	○	○	○	○
Parsley	○	○	○	○	1 Tablespoon	1	0.11g	○	○	○	○
Peas	○	○	○	○	100g	292	24.32g	○	○	○	○
Peppers	○	○	○	○	1 Small Pepper	19	0.73g	○	○	○	○
Poppy Seeds	○	○	○	○	1 Tablespoon	47	1g	○	○	○	○
Potatoes	○	○	○	○	1 Small Potato	131	3.43g	○	○	○	○
Pumpkin Seeds	○	○	○	○	1 Tablespoon	18	4.65g	○	○	○	○
Quinoa	○	○	○	○	100g	143	5.01g	○	○	○	○
Seitan	○	○	○	○	1/3 Cup	120	21g	○	○	○	○
Sesame Seeds	○	○	○	○	1 Tablespoon	52	1.6g	○	○	○	○
Sunflower Seeds	○	○	○	○	1 Tablespoon	55	2g	○	○	○	○
Soba Noodles	○	○	○	○	100g	99	5.06g	○	○	○	○
Soy Protein	○	○	○	○	1 Scoop	55	11.5g	○	○	○	○
Spinach	○	○	○	○	100g	40	2.88g	○	○	○	○
Spirulina	○	○	○	○	1 Tablespoon	25	4g	○	○	○	○
Sprouts	○	○	○	○	100g	29	3.59g	○	○	○	○
Sweet Potato	○	○	○	○	1 Sweet Potato	112	2.04g	○	○	○	○
Tempeh	○	○	○	○	100g	196	18.19g	○	○	○	○
Tofu	○	○	○	○	100g	76	8.08g	○	○	○	○
Watercress	○	○	○	○	100g	11	2.28g	○	○	○	○
Wheat Germ	○	○	○	○	1 Tablespoon	25	2g	○	○	○	○
White Mushrooms	○	○	○	○	1 Small Mushroom	2	0.31g	○	○	○	○

*ALL NUMBERS WILL VARY DEPENDING ON YOUR COOKING METHOD AND SEASONING. USE THIS AS A GENERAL REFERENCE.
**KEEP IN MIND THAT THE AMOUNT OF PROTEIN YOU NEED WILL VARY DEPENDING ON YOUR AGE, WEIGHT AND ACTIVITY LEVEL.

PROTEIN IDEAS
--> More Ideas

- *Protein Bars*
- *Protein Crackers*
- *Protein Pancakes/Waffles*
- *Quesadillas*
- *Quiches*
- *Rice Balls*
- *Risotto/Aranchini*
- *Roasted*
- *Salads*
- *Sandwiches*
- *Sauces/Dips*

baba ganoush
bean dips
cheese dips
guacamole
hummus
chia seed jams
nut/seed dips
pestos
yogurt dips

- *Sausages*
- *Smoothies*
- *Soups*
- *Spring Rolls*
- *Steamed Protein*
- *Stews*
- *Stir Fry*
- *Sushi Rolls*
- *Sushi Sandwiches*
- *Tacos*
- *Taquitos*
- *Trail Mix*
- *Veggie Balls*
- *Wontons*
- *Wraps*

Sweet or Savoury

Sandwich/Wrap/Roll

1. Pick a bread or wrap option...

- ☐ Bagel
- ☐ Baguette
- ☐ Bread
- ☐ Cucumber
- ☐ Crêpe

- ☐ Deli Meat
- ☐ English Muffin
- ☐ Flat Bread
- ☐ Leafy Green
- ☐ Nori

- ☐ Omelete
- ☐ Pancake
- ☐ Phyllo Dough
- ☐ Pita
- ☐ Pizza Dough

- ☐ Rice Paper
- ☐ Sweet Potato Toast
- ☐ Tortilla Wrap
- ☐ Waffle
- ☐ Wonton Sheet

2. Add a spread... (It adds flavor and acts as a "glue" to hold things together)

- ☐ Apple Sauce
- ☐ Avocado
- ☐ BBQ Sauce
- ☐ Butter
- ☐ Chocolate

- ☐ Cream Cheese
- ☐ Honey
- ☐ Hummus
- ☐ Jam
- ☐ Ketchup

- ☐ Mayonnaise
- ☐ Mustard
- ☐ Nut Butters
- ☐ Nut Free Butters
- ☐ Oil & Garlic

- ☐ Pesto
- ☐ Rice (for sushi)
- ☐ Relish
- ☐ Refried Beams
- ☐ Salad Dressing

- ☐ Salsa
- ☐ Tahini
- ☐ Tartar Sauce
- ☐ Tomato Sauce
- ☐ Yogurt

3. Add some extra goodness... (sprinkle it on top of your spread)

- ☐ Chocolate/Cocoa
- ☐ Chia Seeds
- ☐ Flax Seeds

- ☐ Granola
- ☐ Hemp Seeds
- ☐ Herbs

- ☐ Nutritional Yeast
- ☐ Nuts (chopped)
- ☐ Pumpkin Seeds

- ☐ Seasame Seeds
- ☐ Spices
- ☐ Sunflower Seeds

3. Add your toppings...

- ☐ Any leftovers from dinner cut into small pieces or shredded.
- ☐ Beans / Legumes

- ☐ Cheese
- ☐ Meats
- ☐ Eggs
- ☐ Fruit

- ☐ Shrimp
- ☐ Fish
- ☐ Tempeh / Tofu
- ☐ Tuna

- ☐ **Veggies:** Carrots, Corn, Cucumbers, Lettuce, Leafy Greens, Mushrooms, Olives, Onions, Peppers, Pickles, Sprouts, Tomatoes etc.

4. Wrap, roll or add another item from #1.

Slice it up if you want smaller pieces.

5. If needed, Bake or Toast it up.

Let it cool down completely before packing it into a lunch box.

*These ideas will also work for quesadillas, taquitos, empanadas and pizzas.
- Experiment and get creative with your ideas.

Classic PB&J

- 2 pieces of bread
- nut or nut free butter spread
- jam or fresh fruit

Notes:
- also good toasted

Veggie Wrap

- 1 tortilla
- hummus
- cheese
- lettuce & tomato

Notes:
- works as roll too

Sushi Rolls

- 1 sheet of nori
- sticky rice
- sesame seeds
- sliced cucumbers

Notes:
- roll it and slice

*Record your favorite sandwich/wrap/roll combinations for a quick reference.

MY FAVORITE DINNERS
where the leftovers
MAKE GREAT LUNCHES

pizza	tacos	pasta	rice
Turned into:	Turned into:	Turned into:	Turned into:
- Bites	- DIY Tacos	- As is cold	- Fried Rice
- Kabobs/Sticks	- Wraps	- Add to greens	- Sushi Rolls/Balls
- Rolls	- Quesadillas	to make salad	- Sushi Sandwich

*Reinvent leftovers by adding new sauces, fresh ingredients or changing it's shape!

that work *for* LUNCH

HA HA!

waffles	pancakes	oatmeal
Turned into: - Bites/Kabobs - Sandwiches - Sticks	Turned into: - Sandwiches - Cute Shapes - Kabobs	Turned into: - Muffins - Cookies - Bread

"The most remarkable thing about my mother is that for thirty years she served the family nothing but leftovers. The original meal has never been found."

- Calvin Trillin

*Freeze leftover breakfasts for future lunches.

Date: _____   M T W Th F S Su

DRINKS

SNACKS: _____

Recipes & Notes

RATING ☆ ☆ ☆ ☆ ☆

Date: _____   M T W Th F S Su

DRINKS

SNACKS: _____

Recipes & Notes

RATING ☆ ☆ ☆ ☆ ☆

Date: _____   M T W Th F S Su

DRINKS

SNACKS: _____

Recipes & Notes

RATING ☆ ☆ ☆ ☆ ☆

Date: _____   M T W Th F S Su

DRINKS

SNACKS: _____

Recipes & Notes

RATING ☆ ☆ ☆ ☆ ☆

Prepare Ahead ——— WHAT I LIKED...   WHAT I WOULD CHANGE...

☐ I PACKED WHAT I PLANNED   ☐ I MADE SUBSTITUTIONS   ☐ I DIDN'T MAKE A LUNCH

Prepare Ahead ——— WHAT I LIKED...   WHAT I WOULD CHANGE...

☐ I PACKED WHAT I PLANNED   ☐ I MADE SUBSTITUTIONS   ☐ I DIDN'T MAKE A LUNCH

Prepare Ahead ——— WHAT I LIKED...   WHAT I WOULD CHANGE...

☐ I PACKED WHAT I PLANNED   ☐ I MADE SUBSTITUTIONS   ☐ I DIDN'T MAKE A LUNCH

Prepare Ahead ——— WHAT I LIKED...   WHAT I WOULD CHANGE...

☐ I PACKED WHAT I PLANNED   ☐ I MADE SUBSTITUTIONS   ☐ I DIDN'T MAKE A LUNCH

Grocery List

☐
☐
☐
☐
☐
☐
☐
☐
☐
☐
☐
☐
☐
☐
☐
☐
☐
☐
☐
☐
☐
☐

Leftovers /
groceries that
need to be used

✂

"Mom, my friends don't care if my room is messy, they just care if we have food."

Date: _____ M T W Th F S Su

Recipes & Notes

DRINKS

SNACKS:

RATING ☆ ☆ ☆ ☆ ☆

Date: _____ M T W Th F S Su

Recipes & Notes

DRINKS

SNACKS:

RATING ☆ ☆ ☆ ☆ ☆

Date: _____ M T W Th F S Su

Recipes & Notes

DRINKS

SNACKS:

RATING ☆ ☆ ☆ ☆ ☆

Date: _____ M T W Th F S Su

Recipes & Notes

DRINKS

SNACKS:

RATING ☆ ☆ ☆ ☆ ☆

Prepare Ahead — WHAT I LIKED... WHAT I WOULD CHANGE...

☐ I PACKED WHAT I PLANNED   ☐ I MADE SUBSTITUTIONS   ☐ I DIDN'T MAKE A LUNCH

Prepare Ahead — WHAT I LIKED... WHAT I WOULD CHANGE...

☐ I PACKED WHAT I PLANNED   ☐ I MADE SUBSTITUTIONS   ☐ I DIDN'T MAKE A LUNCH

Prepare Ahead — WHAT I LIKED... WHAT I WOULD CHANGE...

☐ I PACKED WHAT I PLANNED   ☐ I MADE SUBSTITUTIONS   ☐ I DIDN'T MAKE A LUNCH

Prepare Ahead — WHAT I LIKED... WHAT I WOULD CHANGE...

☐
☐
☐
☐
☐
☐
☐
☐
☐
☐
☐
☐
☐
☐
☐
☐
☐
☐
☐
☐
☐
☐
☐
☐

Leftovers /
groceries that
need to be used

☐ I PACKED WHAT I PLANNED   ☐ I MADE SUBSTITUTIONS   ☐ I DIDN'T MAKE A LUNCH

"There should be a calorie refund for things that didn't taste as good as you expected."

Date: M T W Th F S Su

Recipes & Notes

DRINKS

SNACKS:

RATING ☆ ☆ ☆ ☆ ☆

Date: M T W Th F S Su

Recipes & Notes

DRINKS

SNACKS:

RATING ☆ ☆ ☆ ☆ ☆

Date: M T W Th F S Su

Recipes & Notes

DRINKS

SNACKS:

RATING ☆ ☆ ☆ ☆ ☆

Date: M T W Th F S Su

Recipes & Notes

DRINKS

SNACKS:

RATING ☆ ☆ ☆ ☆ ☆

Prepare Ahead ——— WHAT I LIKED...   WHAT I WOULD CHANGE...

☐ I PACKED WHAT I PLANNED   ☐ I MADE SUBSTITUTIONS   ☐ I DIDN'T MAKE A LUNCH

Prepare Ahead ——— WHAT I LIKED...   WHAT I WOULD CHANGE...

☐ I PACKED WHAT I PLANNED   ☐ I MADE SUBSTITUTIONS   ☐ I DIDN'T MAKE A LUNCH

Prepare Ahead ——— WHAT I LIKED...   WHAT I WOULD CHANGE...

☐ I PACKED WHAT I PLANNED   ☐ I MADE SUBSTITUTIONS   ☐ I DIDN'T MAKE A LUNCH

Prepare Ahead ——— WHAT I LIKED...   WHAT I WOULD CHANGE...

☐ I PACKED WHAT I PLANNED   ☐ I MADE SUBSTITUTIONS   ☐ I DIDN'T MAKE A LUNCH

Grocery List

☐
☐
☐
☐
☐
☐
☐
☐
☐
☐
☐
☐
☐
☐
☐
☐
☐
☐
☐
☐
☐
☐
☐
☐
☐

Leftovers / groceries that need to be used

✂

"To eat is a necessity, but to eat intelligently is an art." – La Rochefoucauld

Date: _____ M T W Th F S Su

Recipes & Notes

DRINKS

SNACKS: _____

RATING ☆ ☆ ☆ ☆ ☆

Date: _____ M T W Th F S Su

Recipes & Notes

DRINKS

SNACKS: _____

RATING ☆ ☆ ☆ ☆ ☆

Date: _____ M T W Th F S Su

Recipes & Notes

DRINKS

SNACKS: _____

RATING ☆ ☆ ☆ ☆ ☆

Date: _____ M T W Th F S Su

Recipes & Notes

DRINKS

SNACKS: _____

RATING ☆ ☆ ☆ ☆ ☆

Prepare Ahead ——— WHAT I LIKED...   WHAT I WOULD CHANGE...

☐ I PACKED WHAT I PLANNED   ☐ I MADE SUBSTITUTIONS   ☐ I DIDN'T MAKE A LUNCH

Prepare Ahead ——— WHAT I LIKED...   WHAT I WOULD CHANGE...

☐ I PACKED WHAT I PLANNED   ☐ I MADE SUBSTITUTIONS   ☐ I DIDN'T MAKE A LUNCH

Prepare Ahead ——— WHAT I LIKED...   WHAT I WOULD CHANGE...

☐ I PACKED WHAT I PLANNED   ☐ I MADE SUBSTITUTIONS   ☐ I DIDN'T MAKE A LUNCH

Prepare Ahead ——— WHAT I LIKED...   WHAT I WOULD CHANGE...

☐ I PACKED WHAT I PLANNED   ☐ I MADE SUBSTITUTIONS   ☐ I DIDN'T MAKE A LUNCH

Grocery List

☐
☐
☐
☐
☐
☐
☐
☐
☐
☐
☐
☐
☐
☐
☐
☐
☐
☐
☐
☐
☐
☐

Leftovers /
groceries that
need to be used

✂

Date: _____   M T W Th F S Su   *Recipes & Notes*

DRINKS

SNACKS:

RATING ☆ ☆ ☆ ☆ ☆

Date: _____   M T W Th F S Su   *Recipes & Notes*

DRINKS

SNACKS:

RATING ☆ ☆ ☆ ☆ ☆

Date: _____   M T W Th F S Su   *Recipes & Notes*

DRINKS

SNACKS:

RATING ☆ ☆ ☆ ☆ ☆

Date: _____   M T W Th F S Su   *Recipes & Notes*

DRINKS

SNACKS:

RATING ☆ ☆ ☆ ☆ ☆

Prepare Ahead WHAT I LIKED... WHAT I WOULD CHANGE...

☐ I PACKED WHAT I PLANNED ☐ I MADE SUBSTITUTIONS ☐ I DIDN'T MAKE A LUNCH

☐
☐
☐
☐
☐

Prepare Ahead WHAT I LIKED... WHAT I WOULD CHANGE...

☐
☐
☐
☐
☐
☐
☐
☐
☐

☐ I PACKED WHAT I PLANNED ☐ I MADE SUBSTITUTIONS ☐ I DIDN'T MAKE A LUNCH

☐
☐

Prepare Ahead WHAT I LIKED... WHAT I WOULD CHANGE...

☐
☐
☐
☐
☐
☐
☐
☐

☐ I PACKED WHAT I PLANNED ☐ I MADE SUBSTITUTIONS ☐ I DIDN'T MAKE A LUNCH

☐

Prepare Ahead WHAT I LIKED... WHAT I WOULD CHANGE...

Leftovers /
groceries that
need to be used

✂

☐ I PACKED WHAT I PLANNED ☐ I MADE SUBSTITUTIONS ☐ I DIDN'T MAKE A LUNCH

41

"Eat healthy, feel healthy. Eat bad, feel bad."

Date: _____ M T W Th F S Su

Recipes & Notes

DRINKS

SNACKS:

RATING ☆ ☆ ☆ ☆ ☆

Date: _____ M T W Th F S Su

Recipes & Notes

DRINKS

SNACKS:

RATING ☆ ☆ ☆ ☆ ☆

Date: _____ M T W Th F S Su

Recipes & Notes

DRINKS

SNACKS:

RATING ☆ ☆ ☆ ☆ ☆

Date: _____ M T W Th F S Su

Recipes & Notes

DRINKS

SNACKS:

RATING ☆ ☆ ☆ ☆ ☆

Prepare Ahead — WHAT I LIKED... WHAT I WOULD CHANGE...

☐ I PACKED WHAT I PLANNED   ☐ I MADE SUBSTITUTIONS   ☐ I DIDN'T MAKE A LUNCH

Prepare Ahead — WHAT I LIKED... WHAT I WOULD CHANGE...

☐ I PACKED WHAT I PLANNED   ☐ I MADE SUBSTITUTIONS   ☐ I DIDN'T MAKE A LUNCH

Prepare Ahead — WHAT I LIKED... WHAT I WOULD CHANGE...

☐ I PACKED WHAT I PLANNED   ☐ I MADE SUBSTITUTIONS   ☐ I DIDN'T MAKE A LUNCH

Prepare Ahead — WHAT I LIKED... WHAT I WOULD CHANGE...

☐ I PACKED WHAT I PLANNED   ☐ I MADE SUBSTITUTIONS   ☐ I DIDN'T MAKE A LUNCH

Grocery List

☐
☐
☐
☐
☐
☐
☐
☐
☐
☐
☐
☐
☐
☐
☐
☐
☐
☐
☐
☐
☐
☐
☐
☐

Leftovers / groceries that need to be used

"If you don't recognize an ingredient, your body won't either."

Date: _____ M T W Th F S Su

DRINKS

SNACKS:

RATING ☆ ☆ ☆ ☆ ☆

Recipes & Notes

Date: _____ M T W Th F S Su

DRINKS

SNACKS:

RATING ☆ ☆ ☆ ☆ ☆

Recipes & Notes

Date: _____ M T W Th F S Su

DRINKS

SNACKS:

RATING ☆ ☆ ☆ ☆ ☆

Recipes & Notes

Date: _____ M T W Th F S Su

DRINKS

SNACKS:

RATING ☆ ☆ ☆ ☆ ☆

Recipes & Notes

Prepare Ahead — WHAT I LIKED...   WHAT I WOULD CHANGE...

☐ I PACKED WHAT I PLANNED   ☐ I MADE SUBSTITUTIONS   ☐ I DIDN'T MAKE A LUNCH

Prepare Ahead — WHAT I LIKED...   WHAT I WOULD CHANGE...

☐ I PACKED WHAT I PLANNED   ☐ I MADE SUBSTITUTIONS   ☐ I DIDN'T MAKE A LUNCH

Prepare Ahead — WHAT I LIKED...   WHAT I WOULD CHANGE...

☐ I PACKED WHAT I PLANNED   ☐ I MADE SUBSTITUTIONS   ☐ I DIDN'T MAKE A LUNCH

Prepare Ahead — WHAT I LIKED...   WHAT I WOULD CHANGE...

☐ I PACKED WHAT I PLANNED   ☐ I MADE SUBSTITUTIONS   ☐ I DIDN'T MAKE A LUNCH

Grocery List

☐
☐
☐
☐
☐
☐
☐
☐
☐
☐
☐
☐
☐
☐
☐
☐
☐
☐
☐
☐

Leftovers /
groceries that
need to be used

45

Date: _____   M T W Th F S Su

DRINKS

SNACKS:

Recipes & Notes

RATING ☆ ☆ ☆ ☆ ☆

Date: _____   M T W Th F S Su

DRINKS

SNACKS:

Recipes & Notes

RATING ☆ ☆ ☆ ☆ ☆

Date: _____   M T W Th F S Su

DRINKS

SNACKS:

Recipes & Notes

RATING ☆ ☆ ☆ ☆ ☆

Date: _____   M T W Th F S Su

DRINKS

SNACKS:

Recipes & Notes

RATING ☆ ☆ ☆ ☆ ☆

Prepare Ahead ——— WHAT I LIKED...   WHAT I WOULD CHANGE...

☐ I PACKED WHAT I PLANNED   ☐ I MADE SUBSTITUTIONS   ☐ I DIDN'T MAKE A LUNCH

Prepare Ahead ——— WHAT I LIKED...   WHAT I WOULD CHANGE...

☐ I PACKED WHAT I PLANNED   ☐ I MADE SUBSTITUTIONS   ☐ I DIDN'T MAKE A LUNCH

Prepare Ahead ——— WHAT I LIKED...   WHAT I WOULD CHANGE...

☐ I PACKED WHAT I PLANNED   ☐ I MADE SUBSTITUTIONS   ☐ I DIDN'T MAKE A LUNCH

Prepare Ahead ——— WHAT I LIKED...   WHAT I WOULD CHANGE...

☐ I PACKED WHAT I PLANNED   ☐ I MADE SUBSTITUTIONS   ☐ I DIDN'T MAKE A LUNCH

Grocery List

☐
☐
☐
☐
☐
☐
☐
☐
☐
☐
☐
☐
☐
☐
☐
☐
☐
☐
☐
☐
☐
☐

Leftovers /
groceries that
need to be used

✂

47

"The wonderful thing about food is you get three votes a day. Every one of them has the potential to change the world." – Michael Pollan

Date: _____ M T W Th F S Su

Recipes & Notes

DRINKS

SNACKS:

RATING ☆ ☆ ☆ ☆ ☆

Date: _____ M T W Th F S Su

Recipes & Notes

DRINKS

SNACKS:

RATING ☆ ☆ ☆ ☆ ☆

Date: _____ M T W Th F S Su

Recipes & Notes

DRINKS

SNACKS:

RATING ☆ ☆ ☆ ☆ ☆

Date: _____ M T W Th F S Su

Recipes & Notes

DRINKS

SNACKS:

RATING ☆ ☆ ☆ ☆ ☆

Prepare Ahead ——— WHAT I LIKED...   WHAT I WOULD CHANGE...

☐ I PACKED WHAT I PLANNED   ☐ I MADE SUBSTITUTIONS   ☐ I DIDN'T MAKE A LUNCH

Prepare Ahead ——— WHAT I LIKED...   WHAT I WOULD CHANGE...

☐ I PACKED WHAT I PLANNED   ☐ I MADE SUBSTITUTIONS   ☐ I DIDN'T MAKE A LUNCH

Prepare Ahead ——— WHAT I LIKED...   WHAT I WOULD CHANGE...

☐ I PACKED WHAT I PLANNED   ☐ I MADE SUBSTITUTIONS   ☐ I DIDN'T MAKE A LUNCH

Prepare Ahead ——— WHAT I LIKED...   WHAT I WOULD CHANGE...

☐ I PACKED WHAT I PLANNED   ☐ I MADE SUBSTITUTIONS   ☐ I DIDN'T MAKE A LUNCH

Grocery List

☐
☐
☐
☐
☐
☐
☐
☐
☐
☐
☐
☐
☐
☐
☐
☐
☐
☐
☐
☐
☐
☐
☐

Leftovers /
groceries that
need to be used

✂

Date: M T W Th F S Su   *Recipes & Notes*

DRINKS

SNACKS:

RATING ☆ ☆ ☆ ☆ ☆

Date: M T W Th F S Su   *Recipes & Notes*

DRINKS

SNACKS:

RATING ☆ ☆ ☆ ☆ ☆

Date: M T W Th F S Su   *Recipes & Notes*

DRINKS

SNACKS:

RATING ☆ ☆ ☆ ☆ ☆

Date: M T W Th F S Su   *Recipes & Notes*

DRINKS

SNACKS:

RATING ☆ ☆ ☆ ☆ ☆

Prepare Ahead — WHAT I LIKED... WHAT I WOULD CHANGE...

☐ I PACKED WHAT I PLANNED   ☐ I MADE SUBSTITUTIONS   ☐ I DIDN'T MAKE A LUNCH

Prepare Ahead — WHAT I LIKED... WHAT I WOULD CHANGE...

☐ I PACKED WHAT I PLANNED   ☐ I MADE SUBSTITUTIONS   ☐ I DIDN'T MAKE A LUNCH

Prepare Ahead — WHAT I LIKED... WHAT I WOULD CHANGE...

☐ I PACKED WHAT I PLANNED   ☐ I MADE SUBSTITUTIONS   ☐ I DIDN'T MAKE A LUNCH

Prepare Ahead — WHAT I LIKED... WHAT I WOULD CHANGE...

☐ I PACKED WHAT I PLANNED   ☐ I MADE SUBSTITUTIONS   ☐ I DIDN'T MAKE A LUNCH

Grocery List

☐
☐
☐
☐
☐
☐
☐
☐
☐
☐
☐
☐
☐
☐
☐
☐
☐
☐
☐
☐
☐

Leftovers /
groceries that
need to be used

✂

51

"If you keep good food in your fridge, you will eat good food." – Errick McAdams

Date: _____ M T W Th F S Su

Recipes & Notes

DRINKS

SNACKS:

RATING ☆ ☆ ☆ ☆ ☆

Date: _____ M T W Th F S Su

Recipes & Notes

DRINKS

SNACKS:

RATING ☆ ☆ ☆ ☆ ☆

Date: _____ M T W Th F S Su

Recipes & Notes

DRINKS

SNACKS:

RATING ☆ ☆ ☆ ☆ ☆

Date: _____ M T W Th F S Su

Recipes & Notes

DRINKS

SNACKS:

RATING ☆ ☆ ☆ ☆ ☆

Prepare Ahead ——— WHAT I LIKED...   WHAT I WOULD CHANGE...

☐ I PACKED WHAT I PLANNED   ☐ I MADE SUBSTITUTIONS   ☐ I DIDN'T MAKE A LUNCH

Prepare Ahead ——— WHAT I LIKED...   WHAT I WOULD CHANGE...

☐ I PACKED WHAT I PLANNED   ☐ I MADE SUBSTITUTIONS   ☐ I DIDN'T MAKE A LUNCH

Prepare Ahead ——— WHAT I LIKED...   WHAT I WOULD CHANGE...

☐ I PACKED WHAT I PLANNED   ☐ I MADE SUBSTITUTIONS   ☐ I DIDN'T MAKE A LUNCH

Prepare Ahead ——— WHAT I LIKED...   WHAT I WOULD CHANGE...

☐ I PACKED WHAT I PLANNED   ☐ I MADE SUBSTITUTIONS   ☐ I DIDN'T MAKE A LUNCH

Grocery List

☐
☐
☐
☐
☐
☐
☐
☐
☐
☐
☐
☐
☐
☐
☐
☐
☐
☐
☐
☐
☐
☐
☐
☐

Leftovers / groceries that need to be used

✂

"No one is born a great cook, one learns from doing." – Julia Child

Date: M T W Th F S Su

DRINKS

SNACKS:

Recipes & Notes

RATING ☆ ☆ ☆ ☆ ☆

Date: M T W Th F S Su

DRINKS

SNACKS:

Recipes & Notes

RATING ☆ ☆ ☆ ☆ ☆

Date: M T W Th F S Su

DRINKS

SNACKS:

Recipes & Notes

RATING ☆ ☆ ☆ ☆ ☆

Date: M T W Th F S Su

DRINKS

SNACKS:

Recipes & Notes

RATING ☆ ☆ ☆ ☆ ☆

Prepare Ahead — WHAT I LIKED...   WHAT I WOULD CHANGE...

☐ I PACKED WHAT I PLANNED   ☐ I MADE SUBSTITUTIONS   ☐ I DIDN'T MAKE A LUNCH

Prepare Ahead — WHAT I LIKED...   WHAT I WOULD CHANGE...

☐ I PACKED WHAT I PLANNED   ☐ I MADE SUBSTITUTIONS   ☐ I DIDN'T MAKE A LUNCH

Prepare Ahead — WHAT I LIKED...   WHAT I WOULD CHANGE...

☐ I PACKED WHAT I PLANNED   ☐ I MADE SUBSTITUTIONS   ☐ I DIDN'T MAKE A LUNCH

Prepare Ahead — WHAT I LIKED...   WHAT I WOULD CHANGE...

☐ I PACKED WHAT I PLANNED   ☐ I MADE SUBSTITUTIONS   ☐ I DIDN'T MAKE A LUNCH

Grocery List

☐
☐
☐
☐
☐
☐
☐
☐
☐
☐
☐
☐
☐
☐
☐
☐
☐
☐
☐
☐
☐
☐
☐
☐

Leftovers /
groceries that
need to be used

✂

"Love and food – it is all about spice."

Date: _____ M T W Th F S Su *Recipes & Notes*

DRINKS

SNACKS:

RATING ☆ ☆ ☆ ☆ ☆

Date: _____ M T W Th F S Su *Recipes & Notes*

DRINKS

SNACKS:

RATING ☆ ☆ ☆ ☆ ☆

Date: _____ M T W Th F S Su *Recipes & Notes*

DRINKS

SNACKS:

RATING ☆ ☆ ☆ ☆ ☆

Date: _____ M T W Th F S Su *Recipes & Notes*

DRINKS

SNACKS:

RATING ☆ ☆ ☆ ☆ ☆

Prepare Ahead — WHAT I LIKED...   WHAT I WOULD CHANGE...

☐ I PACKED WHAT I PLANNED   ☐ I MADE SUBSTITUTIONS   ☐ I DIDN'T MAKE A LUNCH

Prepare Ahead — WHAT I LIKED...   WHAT I WOULD CHANGE...

☐ I PACKED WHAT I PLANNED   ☐ I MADE SUBSTITUTIONS   ☐ I DIDN'T MAKE A LUNCH

Prepare Ahead — WHAT I LIKED...   WHAT I WOULD CHANGE...

☐ I PACKED WHAT I PLANNED   ☐ I MADE SUBSTITUTIONS   ☐ I DIDN'T MAKE A LUNCH

Prepare Ahead — WHAT I LIKED...   WHAT I WOULD CHANGE...

☐ I PACKED WHAT I PLANNED   ☐ I MADE SUBSTITUTIONS   ☐ I DIDN'T MAKE A LUNCH

Grocery List

☐
☐
☐
☐
☐
☐
☐
☐
☐
☐
☐
☐
☐
☐
☐
☐
☐
☐
☐
☐
☐
☐
☐
☐

Leftovers /
groceries that
need to be used

✂

"It is more fun to talk with someone who doesn't use long, difficult words but rather short, easy words like "what about lunch?" - A.A. Milne

Date: M T W Th F S Su   *Recipes & Notes*

DRINKS

SNACKS:

RATING ☆ ☆ ☆ ☆ ☆

Date: M T W Th F S Su   *Recipes & Notes*

DRINKS

SNACKS:

RATING ☆ ☆ ☆ ☆ ☆

Date: M T W Th F S Su   *Recipes & Notes*

DRINKS

SNACKS:

RATING ☆ ☆ ☆ ☆ ☆

Date: M T W Th F S Su   *Recipes & Notes*

DRINKS

SNACKS:

RATING ☆ ☆ ☆ ☆ ☆

Prepare Ahead ———— WHAT I LIKED...   WHAT I WOULD CHANGE...

☐ I PACKED WHAT I PLANNED   ☐ I MADE SUBSTITUTIONS   ☐ I DIDN'T MAKE A LUNCH

Prepare Ahead ———— WHAT I LIKED...   WHAT I WOULD CHANGE...

☐ I PACKED WHAT I PLANNED   ☐ I MADE SUBSTITUTIONS   ☐ I DIDN'T MAKE A LUNCH

Prepare Ahead ———— WHAT I LIKED...   WHAT I WOULD CHANGE...

☐ I PACKED WHAT I PLANNED   ☐ I MADE SUBSTITUTIONS   ☐ I DIDN'T MAKE A LUNCH

Prepare Ahead ———— WHAT I LIKED...   WHAT I WOULD CHANGE...

☐ I PACKED WHAT I PLANNED   ☐ I MADE SUBSTITUTIONS   ☐ I DIDN'T MAKE A LUNCH

Grocery List

☐
☐
☐
☐
☐
☐
☐
☐
☐
☐
☐
☐
☐
☐
☐
☐
☐
☐
☐
☐
☐
☐
☐

Leftovers / groceries that need to be used

"We all eat, and it would be a sad waste of opportunity to eat badly." – Anna Thomas

Date: _____ M T W Th F S Su

DRINKS

SNACKS:

RATING ☆ ☆ ☆ ☆ ☆

Date: _____ M T W Th F S Su

DRINKS

SNACKS:

Recipes & Notes

RATING ☆ ☆ ☆ ☆ ☆

Date: _____ M T W Th F S Su

DRINKS

SNACKS:

Recipes & Notes

RATING ☆ ☆ ☆ ☆ ☆

Date: _____ M T W Th F S Su

DRINKS

SNACKS:

Recipes & Notes

RATING ☆ ☆ ☆ ☆ ☆

Prepare Ahead WHAT I LIKED... WHAT I WOULD CHANGE...

☐ I PACKED WHAT I PLANNED   ☐ I MADE SUBSTITUTIONS   ☐ I DIDN'T MAKE A LUNCH

Prepare Ahead WHAT I LIKED... WHAT I WOULD CHANGE...

☐ I PACKED WHAT I PLANNED   ☐ I MADE SUBSTITUTIONS   ☐ I DIDN'T MAKE A LUNCH

Prepare Ahead WHAT I LIKED... WHAT I WOULD CHANGE...

☐ I PACKED WHAT I PLANNED   ☐ I MADE SUBSTITUTIONS   ☐ I DIDN'T MAKE A LUNCH

Prepare Ahead WHAT I LIKED... WHAT I WOULD CHANGE...

☐ I PACKED WHAT I PLANNED   ☐ I MADE SUBSTITUTIONS   ☐ I DIDN'T MAKE A LUNCH

Grocery List

☐
☐
☐
☐
☐
☐
☐
☐
☐
☐
☐
☐
☐
☐
☐
☐
☐
☐
☐
☐
☐
☐
☐

Leftovers / groceries that need to be used

"What could be more important than a little something to eat?" – Winnie the Pooh

Date: _____ M T W Th F S Su

DRINKS

SNACKS:

RATING ☆ ☆ ☆ ☆ ☆

Date: _____ M T W Th F S Su

DRINKS

SNACKS:

RATING ☆ ☆ ☆ ☆ ☆

Date: _____ M T W Th F S Su

DRINKS

SNACKS:

RATING ☆ ☆ ☆ ☆ ☆

Date: _____ M T W Th F S Su

DRINKS

SNACKS:

RATING ☆ ☆ ☆ ☆ ☆

Prepare Ahead ——————— WHAT I LIKED...   WHAT I WOULD CHANGE...

☐ I PACKED WHAT I PLANNED   ☐ I MADE SUBSTITUTIONS   ☐ I DIDN'T MAKE A LUNCH

Prepare Ahead ——————— WHAT I LIKED...   WHAT I WOULD CHANGE...

☐ I PACKED WHAT I PLANNED   ☐ I MADE SUBSTITUTIONS   ☐ I DIDN'T MAKE A LUNCH

Prepare Ahead ——————— WHAT I LIKED...   WHAT I WOULD CHANGE...

☐ I PACKED WHAT I PLANNED   ☐ I MADE SUBSTITUTIONS   ☐ I DIDN'T MAKE A LUNCH

Prepare Ahead ——————— WHAT I LIKED...   WHAT I WOULD CHANGE...

☐ I PACKED WHAT I PLANNED   ☐ I MADE SUBSTITUTIONS   ☐ I DIDN'T MAKE A LUNCH

Grocery List

☐
☐
☐
☐
☐
☐
☐
☐
☐
☐
☐
☐
☐
☐
☐
☐
☐
☐
☐
☐
☐
☐

Leftovers /
groceries that
need to be used

"Let food be thy medicine and medicine be thy food." – Hippocrates

Date: _____ M T W Th F S Su

Recipes & Notes

DRINKS

SNACKS:

RATING ☆ ☆ ☆ ☆ ☆

Date: _____ M T W Th F S Su

Recipes & Notes

DRINKS

SNACKS:

RATING ☆ ☆ ☆ ☆ ☆

Date: _____ M T W Th F S Su

Recipes & Notes

DRINKS

SNACKS:

RATING ☆ ☆ ☆ ☆ ☆

Date: _____ M T W Th F S Su

Recipes & Notes

DRINKS

SNACKS:

RATING ☆ ☆ ☆ ☆ ☆

Prepare Ahead — WHAT I LIKED...   WHAT I WOULD CHANGE...

☐ I PACKED WHAT I PLANNED   ☐ I MADE SUBSTITUTIONS   ☐ I DIDN'T MAKE A LUNCH

Prepare Ahead — WHAT I LIKED...   WHAT I WOULD CHANGE...

☐ I PACKED WHAT I PLANNED   ☐ I MADE SUBSTITUTIONS   ☐ I DIDN'T MAKE A LUNCH

Prepare Ahead — WHAT I LIKED...   WHAT I WOULD CHANGE...

☐ I PACKED WHAT I PLANNED   ☐ I MADE SUBSTITUTIONS   ☐ I DIDN'T MAKE A LUNCH

Prepare Ahead — WHAT I LIKED...   WHAT I WOULD CHANGE...

☐ I PACKED WHAT I PLANNED   ☐ I MADE SUBSTITUTIONS   ☐ I DIDN'T MAKE A LUNCH

Grocery List

☐
☐
☐
☐
☐
☐
☐
☐
☐
☐
☐
☐
☐
☐
☐
☐
☐
☐
☐
☐
☐
☐
☐
☐

Leftovers /
groceries that
need to be used

✂

Date: _____ M T W Th F S Su

Recipes & Notes

DRINKS

SNACKS: _____

RATING ☆ ☆ ☆ ☆ ☆

Date: _____ M T W Th F S Su

Recipes & Notes

DRINKS

SNACKS: _____

RATING ☆ ☆ ☆ ☆ ☆

Date: _____ M T W Th F S Su

Recipes & Notes

DRINKS

SNACKS: _____

RATING ☆ ☆ ☆ ☆ ☆

Date: _____ M T W Th F S Su

Recipes & Notes

DRINKS

SNACKS: _____

RATING ☆ ☆ ☆ ☆ ☆

Prepare Ahead — WHAT I LIKED... — WHAT I WOULD CHANGE...

☐ I PACKED WHAT I PLANNED ☐ I MADE SUBSTITUTIONS ☐ I DIDN'T MAKE A LUNCH

Prepare Ahead — WHAT I LIKED... — WHAT I WOULD CHANGE...

☐ I PACKED WHAT I PLANNED ☐ I MADE SUBSTITUTIONS ☐ I DIDN'T MAKE A LUNCH

Prepare Ahead — WHAT I LIKED... — WHAT I WOULD CHANGE...

☐ I PACKED WHAT I PLANNED ☐ I MADE SUBSTITUTIONS ☐ I DIDN'T MAKE A LUNCH

Prepare Ahead — WHAT I LIKED... — WHAT I WOULD CHANGE...

☐ I PACKED WHAT I PLANNED ☐ I MADE SUBSTITUTIONS ☐ I DIDN'T MAKE A LUNCH

Grocery List

☐
☐
☐
☐
☐
☐
☐
☐
☐
☐
☐
☐
☐
☐
☐
☐
☐
☐
☐
☐
☐
☐
☐

Leftovers /
groceries that
need to be used

Date: _____ M T W Th F S Su

Recipes & Notes

DRINKS

SNACKS:

RATING ☆ ☆ ☆ ☆ ☆

Date: _____ M T W Th F S Su

Recipes & Notes

DRINKS

SNACKS:

RATING ☆ ☆ ☆ ☆ ☆

Date: _____ M T W Th F S Su

Recipes & Notes

DRINKS

SNACKS:

RATING ☆ ☆ ☆ ☆ ☆

Date: _____ M T W Th F S Su

Recipes & Notes

DRINKS

SNACKS:

RATING ☆ ☆ ☆ ☆ ☆

Prepare Ahead — WHAT I LIKED... WHAT I WOULD CHANGE...

☐ I PACKED WHAT I PLANNED   ☐ I MADE SUBSTITUTIONS   ☐ I DIDN'T MAKE A LUNCH

Prepare Ahead — WHAT I LIKED... WHAT I WOULD CHANGE...

☐ I PACKED WHAT I PLANNED   ☐ I MADE SUBSTITUTIONS   ☐ I DIDN'T MAKE A LUNCH

Prepare Ahead — WHAT I LIKED... WHAT I WOULD CHANGE...

☐ I PACKED WHAT I PLANNED   ☐ I MADE SUBSTITUTIONS   ☐ I DIDN'T MAKE A LUNCH

Prepare Ahead — WHAT I LIKED... WHAT I WOULD CHANGE...

☐
☐
☐
☐
☐
☐
☐
☐
☐
☐
☐
☐
☐
☐
☐
☐
☐
☐
☐
☐
☐
☐
☐
☐
☐

Leftovers /
groceries that
need to be used

✂

☐ I PACKED WHAT I PLANNED   ☐ I MADE SUBSTITUTIONS   ☐ I DIDN'T MAKE A LUNCH

Date: _____ M T W Th F S Su

Recipes & Notes

DRINKS

SNACKS:

RATING ☆ ☆ ☆ ☆ ☆

Date: _____ M T W Th F S Su

Recipes & Notes

DRINKS

SNACKS:

RATING ☆ ☆ ☆ ☆ ☆

Date: _____ M T W Th F S Su

Recipes & Notes

DRINKS

SNACKS:

- RATING ☆ ☆ ☆ ☆ ☆

Date: _____ M T W Th F S Su

Recipes & Notes

DRINKS

SNACKS:

RATING ☆ ☆ ☆ ☆ ☆

—— *Prepare Ahead* —— WHAT I LIKED...   WHAT I WOULD CHANGE...

☐
☐
☐
☐
☐
☐
☐

☐ I PACKED WHAT I PLANNED ☐ I MADE SUBSTITUTIONS ☐ I DIDN'T MAKE A LUNCH

—— *Prepare Ahead* —— WHAT I LIKED...   WHAT I WOULD CHANGE...

☐
☐
☐
☐
☐
☐

☐ I PACKED WHAT I PLANNED ☐ I MADE SUBSTITUTIONS ☐ I DIDN'T MAKE A LUNCH

—— *Prepare Ahead* —— WHAT I LIKED...   WHAT I WOULD CHANGE...

☐
☐
☐
☐
☐
☐
☐
☐

☐ I PACKED WHAT I PLANNED ☐ I MADE SUBSTITUTIONS ☐ I DIDN'T MAKE A LUNCH

—— *Prepare Ahead* —— WHAT I LIKED...   WHAT I WOULD CHANGE...

Leftovers /
groceries that
need to be used

✂

☐ I PACKED WHAT I PLANNED ☐ I MADE SUBSTITUTIONS ☐ I DIDN'T MAKE A LUNCH

Date: M T W Th F S Su

Recipes & Notes

DRINKS

SNACKS:

RATING ☆ ☆ ☆ ☆ ☆

Date: M T W Th F S Su

Recipes & Notes

DRINKS

SNACKS:

RATING ☆ ☆ ☆ ☆ ☆

Date: M T W Th F S Su

Recipes & Notes

DRINKS

SNACKS:

RATING ☆ ☆ ☆ ☆ ☆

Date: M T W Th F S Su

Recipes & Notes

DRINKS

SNACKS:

RATING ☆ ☆ ☆ ☆ ☆

Prepare Ahead — WHAT I LIKED... — WHAT I WOULD CHANGE...

☐ I PACKED WHAT I PLANNED   ☐ I MADE SUBSTITUTIONS   ☐ I DIDN'T MAKE A LUNCH

Prepare Ahead — WHAT I LIKED... — WHAT I WOULD CHANGE...

☐ I PACKED WHAT I PLANNED   ☐ I MADE SUBSTITUTIONS   ☐ I DIDN'T MAKE A LUNCH

Prepare Ahead — WHAT I LIKED... — WHAT I WOULD CHANGE...

☐ I PACKED WHAT I PLANNED   ☐ I MADE SUBSTITUTIONS   ☐ I DIDN'T MAKE A LUNCH

Prepare Ahead — WHAT I LIKED... — WHAT I WOULD CHANGE...

☐ I PACKED WHAT I PLANNED   ☐ I MADE SUBSTITUTIONS   ☐ I DIDN'T MAKE A LUNCH

Grocery List

☐
☐
☐
☐
☐
☐
☐
☐
☐
☐
☐
☐
☐
☐
☐
☐
☐
☐
☐
☐
☐
☐

Leftovers /
groceries that
need to be used

"Vegetables are a must on a diet. I suggest carrot cake, zucchini bread, and pumpkin pie."

– Jim Davis

Date: _____ M T W Th F S Su

DRINKS

SNACKS:

Recipes & Notes

RATING ☆ ☆ ☆ ☆ ☆

Date: _____ M T W Th F S Su

DRINKS

SNACKS:

Recipes & Notes

RATING ☆ ☆ ☆ ☆ ☆

Date: _____ M T W Th F S Su

DRINKS

SNACKS:

Recipes & Notes

RATING ☆ ☆ ☆ ☆ ☆

Date: _____ M T W Th F S Su

DRINKS

SNACKS:

Recipes & Notes

RATING ☆ ☆ ☆ ☆ ☆

Prepare Ahead — WHAT I LIKED... — WHAT I WOULD CHANGE...

☐ I PACKED WHAT I PLANNED   ☐ I MADE SUBSTITUTIONS   ☐ I DIDN'T MAKE A LUNCH

Prepare Ahead — WHAT I LIKED... — WHAT I WOULD CHANGE...

☐ I PACKED WHAT I PLANNED   ☐ I MADE SUBSTITUTIONS   ☐ I DIDN'T MAKE A LUNCH

Prepare Ahead — WHAT I LIKED... — WHAT I WOULD CHANGE...

☐ I PACKED WHAT I PLANNED   ☐ I MADE SUBSTITUTIONS   ☐ I DIDN'T MAKE A LUNCH

Prepare Ahead — WHAT I LIKED... — WHAT I WOULD CHANGE...

☐ I PACKED WHAT I PLANNED   ☐ I MADE SUBSTITUTIONS   ☐ I DIDN'T MAKE A LUNCH

Grocery List

☐
☐
☐
☐
☐
☐
☐
☐
☐
☐
☐
☐
☐
☐
☐
☐
☐
☐
☐
☐
☐

Leftovers / groceries that need to be used

✂

"The most indispensable ingredient of all good home cooking: love for those you are cooking for."
— Sophia Loren

Date: _____   M   T   W   Th   F   S   Su

DRINKS

SNACKS: _____

RATING ☆ ☆ ☆ ☆ ☆

Date: _____   M   T   W   Th   F   S   Su

Recipes & Notes

DRINKS

SNACKS: _____

RATING ☆ ☆ ☆ ☆ ☆

Date: _____   M   T   W   Th   F   S   Su

Recipes & Notes

DRINKS

SNACKS: _____

RATING ☆ ☆ ☆ ☆ ☆

Date: _____   M   T   W   Th   F   S   Su

Recipes & Notes

DRINKS

SNACKS: _____

RATING ☆ ☆ ☆ ☆ ☆

Prepare Ahead — WHAT I LIKED...   WHAT I WOULD CHANGE...

☐
☐
☐
☐
☐
☐
☐
☐
☐
☐
☐
☐
☐
☐
☐

☐ I PACKED WHAT I PLANNED   ☐ I MADE SUBSTITUTIONS   ☐ I DIDN'T MAKE A LUNCH

Prepare Ahead — WHAT I LIKED...   WHAT I WOULD CHANGE...

☐ I PACKED WHAT I PLANNED   ☐ I MADE SUBSTITUTIONS   ☐ I DIDN'T MAKE A LUNCH

Prepare Ahead — WHAT I LIKED...   WHAT I WOULD CHANGE...

☐
☐
☐
☐
☐
☐
☐

☐ I PACKED WHAT I PLANNED   ☐ I MADE SUBSTITUTIONS   ☐ I DIDN'T MAKE A LUNCH

Prepare Ahead — WHAT I LIKED...   WHAT I WOULD CHANGE...

Leftovers /
groceries that
need to be used

✂

☐ I PACKED WHAT I PLANNED   ☐ I MADE SUBSTITUTIONS   ☐ I DIDN'T MAKE A LUNCH

"Cupcakes are muffins that believed in miracles."

Date: _____ M T W Th F S Su

Recipes & Notes

DRINKS

SNACKS:

RATING ☆ ☆ ☆ ☆ ☆

Date: _____ M T W Th F S Su

Recipes & Notes

DRINKS

SNACKS:

RATING ☆ ☆ ☆ ☆ ☆

Date: _____ M T W Th F S Su

Recipes & Notes

DRINKS

SNACKS:

RATING ☆ ☆ ☆ ☆ ☆

Date: _____ M T W Th F S Su

Recipes & Notes

DRINKS

SNACKS:

RATING ☆ ☆ ☆ ☆ ☆

Prepare Ahead WHAT I LIKED... WHAT I WOULD CHANGE...

☐ I PACKED WHAT I PLANNED   ☐ I MADE SUBSTITUTIONS   ☐ I DIDN'T MAKE A LUNCH

Prepare Ahead WHAT I LIKED... WHAT I WOULD CHANGE...

☐ I PACKED WHAT I PLANNED   ☐ I MADE SUBSTITUTIONS   ☐ I DIDN'T MAKE A LUNCH

Prepare Ahead WHAT I LIKED... WHAT I WOULD CHANGE...

☐ I PACKED WHAT I PLANNED   ☐ I MADE SUBSTITUTIONS   ☐ I DIDN'T MAKE A LUNCH

Prepare Ahead WHAT I LIKED... WHAT I WOULD CHANGE...

☐ I PACKED WHAT I PLANNED   ☐ I MADE SUBSTITUTIONS   ☐ I DIDN'T MAKE A LUNCH

Grocery List

☐
☐
☐
☐
☐
☐
☐
☐
☐
☐
☐
☐
☐
☐
☐
☐
☐
☐
☐
☐
☐
☐
☐

Leftovers / groceries that need to be used

✂

"Tell me what you eat, and I will tell you who you are." – Jean Anthem Brillat-Savarin

Date: _____ M T W Th F S Su

Recipes & Notes

DRINKS

SNACKS:

RATING ☆ ☆ ☆ ☆ ☆

Date: _____ M T W Th F S Su

Recipes & Notes

DRINKS

SNACKS:

RATING ☆ ☆ ☆ ☆ ☆

Date: _____ M T W Th F S Su

Recipes & Notes

DRINKS

SNACKS:

RATING ☆ ☆ ☆ ☆ ☆

Date: _____ M T W Th F S Su

Recipes & Notes

DRINKS

SNACKS:

RATING ☆ ☆ ☆ ☆ ☆

Prepare Ahead — WHAT I LIKED...   WHAT I WOULD CHANGE...

☐ I PACKED WHAT I PLANNED   ☐ I MADE SUBSTITUTIONS   ☐ I DIDN'T MAKE A LUNCH

Prepare Ahead — WHAT I LIKED...   WHAT I WOULD CHANGE...

☐ I PACKED WHAT I PLANNED   ☐ I MADE SUBSTITUTIONS   ☐ I DIDN'T MAKE A LUNCH

Prepare Ahead — WHAT I LIKED...   WHAT I WOULD CHANGE...

☐ I PACKED WHAT I PLANNED   ☐ I MADE SUBSTITUTIONS   ☐ I DIDN'T MAKE A LUNCH

Prepare Ahead — WHAT I LIKED...   WHAT I WOULD CHANGE...

☐ I PACKED WHAT I PLANNED   ☐ I MADE SUBSTITUTIONS   ☐ I DIDN'T MAKE A LUNCH

Grocery List

☐
☐
☐
☐
☐
☐
☐
☐
☐
☐
☐
☐
☐
☐
☐
☐
☐
☐
☐
☐
☐
☐
☐

Leftovers /
groceries that
need to be used

✂

81

"Developing healthy eating habits becomes easier each day."

Date: _____   M   T   W   Th   F   S   Su   *Recipes & Notes*

DRINKS

SNACKS:

RATING ☆ ☆ ☆ ☆ ☆

Date: _____   M   T   W   Th   F   S   Su   *Recipes & Notes*

DRINKS

SNACKS:

RATING ☆ ☆ ☆ ☆ ☆

Date: _____   M   T   W   Th   F   S   Su   *Recipes & Notes*

DRINKS

SNACKS:

RATING ☆ ☆ ☆ ☆ ☆

Date: _____   M   T   W   Th   F   S   Su   *Recipes & Notes*

DRINKS

SNACKS:

RATING ☆ ☆ ☆ ☆ ☆

Prepare Ahead   WHAT I LIKED...   WHAT I WOULD CHANGE...

☐ I PACKED WHAT I PLANNED   ☐ I MADE SUBSTITUTIONS   ☐ I DIDN'T MAKE A LUNCH

Prepare Ahead   WHAT I LIKED...   WHAT I WOULD CHANGE...

☐ I PACKED WHAT I PLANNED   ☐ I MADE SUBSTITUTIONS   ☐ I DIDN'T MAKE A LUNCH

Prepare Ahead   WHAT I LIKED...   WHAT I WOULD CHANGE...

☐ I PACKED WHAT I PLANNED   ☐ I MADE SUBSTITUTIONS   ☐ I DIDN'T MAKE A LUNCH

Prepare Ahead   WHAT I LIKED...   WHAT I WOULD CHANGE...

☐ I PACKED WHAT I PLANNED   ☐ I MADE SUBSTITUTIONS   ☐ I DIDN'T MAKE A LUNCH

Grocery List

☐
☐
☐
☐
☐
☐
☐
☐
☐
☐
☐
☐
☐
☐
☐
☐
☐
☐
☐
☐
☐
☐

Leftovers / groceries that need to be used

"If you can't feed a hundred people, then feed just one." – Mother Teresa

---

Date: _____   M T W Th F S Su

Recipes & Notes

DRINKS

SNACKS: _____

RATING ☆ ☆ ☆ ☆ ☆

Date: _____   M T W Th F S Su

Recipes & Notes

DRINKS

SNACKS: _____

RATING ☆ ☆ ☆ ☆ ☆

Date: _____   M T W Th F S Su

Recipes & Notes

DRINKS

SNACKS: _____

RATING ☆ ☆ ☆ ☆ ☆

Date: _____   M T W Th F S Su

Recipes & Notes

DRINKS

SNACKS: _____

RATING ☆ ☆ ☆ ☆ ☆

Prepare Ahead — WHAT I LIKED... WHAT I WOULD CHANGE...

Grocery List

☐ I PACKED WHAT I PLANNED   ☐ I MADE SUBSTITUTIONS   ☐ I DIDN'T MAKE A LUNCH

☐
☐
☐
☐
☐
☐
☐
☐
☐
☐
☐
☐

Prepare Ahead — WHAT I LIKED... WHAT I WOULD CHANGE...

☐ I PACKED WHAT I PLANNED   ☐ I MADE SUBSTITUTIONS   ☐ I DIDN'T MAKE A LUNCH

☐
☐
☐
☐
☐
☐
☐

Prepare Ahead — WHAT I LIKED... WHAT I WOULD CHANGE...

☐ I PACKED WHAT I PLANNED   ☐ I MADE SUBSTITUTIONS   ☐ I DIDN'T MAKE A LUNCH

☐
☐

Prepare Ahead — WHAT I LIKED... WHAT I WOULD CHANGE...

Leftovers / groceries that need to be used

✂

☐ I PACKED WHAT I PLANNED   ☐ I MADE SUBSTITUTIONS   ☐ I DIDN'T MAKE A LUNCH

85

"The beauty of "food as medicine" is that the choice to heal and promote health can begin as soon as the next meal."

Date: _____   M T W Th F S Su

Recipes & Notes

DRINKS

SNACKS:

RATING ☆ ☆ ☆ ☆ ☆

Date: _____   M T W Th F S Su

Recipes & Notes

DRINKS

SNACKS:

RATING ☆ ☆ ☆ ☆ ☆

Date: _____   M T W Th F S Su

Recipes & Notes

DRINKS

SNACKS:

RATING ☆ ☆ ☆ ☆ ☆

Date: _____   M T W Th F S Su

Recipes & Notes

DRINKS

SNACKS:

RATING ☆ ☆ ☆ ☆ ☆

Prepare Ahead ——— WHAT I LIKED... WHAT I WOULD CHANGE...

☐ I PACKED WHAT I PLANNED ☐ I MADE SUBSTITUTIONS ☐ I DIDN'T MAKE A LUNCH

Prepare Ahead ——— WHAT I LIKED... WHAT I WOULD CHANGE...

☐ I PACKED WHAT I PLANNED ☐ I MADE SUBSTITUTIONS ☐ I DIDN'T MAKE A LUNCH

Prepare Ahead ——— WHAT I LIKED... WHAT I WOULD CHANGE...

☐ I PACKED WHAT I PLANNED ☐ I MADE SUBSTITUTIONS ☐ I DIDN'T MAKE A LUNCH

Prepare Ahead ——— WHAT I LIKED... WHAT I WOULD CHANGE...

☐ I PACKED WHAT I PLANNED ☐ I MADE SUBSTITUTIONS ☐ I DIDN'T MAKE A LUNCH

Grocery List

☐
☐
☐
☐
☐
☐
☐
☐
☐
☐
☐
☐
☐
☐
☐
☐
☐
☐
☐
☐
☐

Leftovers / groceries that need to be used

✂

"The kitchen is a country in which there are always discoveries to be made."
– Grimed de La Beyniere

Date: _____ M T W Th F S Su

DRINKS

SNACKS:

RATING ☆ ☆ ☆ ☆ ☆

Date: _____ M T W Th F S Su

DRINKS

SNACKS:

RATING ☆ ☆ ☆ ☆ ☆

Date: _____ M T W Th F S Su

DRINKS

SNACKS:

RATING ☆ ☆ ☆ ☆ ☆

Date: _____ M T W Th F S Su

DRINKS

SNACKS:

RATING ☆ ☆ ☆ ☆ ☆

Prepare Ahead — WHAT I LIKED...   WHAT I WOULD CHANGE...

☐ I PACKED WHAT I PLANNED   ☐ I MADE SUBSTITUTIONS   ☐ I DIDN'T MAKE A LUNCH

Prepare Ahead — WHAT I LIKED...   WHAT I WOULD CHANGE...

☐ I PACKED WHAT I PLANNED   ☐ I MADE SUBSTITUTIONS   ☐ I DIDN'T MAKE A LUNCH

Prepare Ahead — WHAT I LIKED...   WHAT I WOULD CHANGE...

☐ I PACKED WHAT I PLANNED   ☐ I MADE SUBSTITUTIONS   ☐ I DIDN'T MAKE A LUNCH

Prepare Ahead — WHAT I LIKED...   WHAT I WOULD CHANGE...

☐ I PACKED WHAT I PLANNED   ☐ I MADE SUBSTITUTIONS   ☐ I DIDN'T MAKE A LUNCH

Grocery List

☐
☐
☐
☐
☐
☐
☐
☐
☐
☐
☐
☐
☐
☐
☐
☐
☐
☐
☐
☐
☐
☐
☐

Leftovers /
groceries that
need to be used

"I always make a list before I go to the grocery store. Sometimes, I even remember to bring it with me."

Date: _____ M T W Th F S Su

Recipes & Notes

DRINKS

SNACKS: _____

RATING ☆ ☆ ☆ ☆ ☆

Date: _____ M T W Th F S Su

Recipes & Notes

DRINKS

SNACKS: _____

RATING ☆ ☆ ☆ ☆ ☆

Date: _____ M T W Th F S Su

Recipes & Notes

DRINKS

SNACKS: _____

RATING ☆ ☆ ☆ ☆ ☆

Date: _____ M T W Th F S Su

Recipes & Notes

DRINKS

SNACKS: _____

RATING ☆ ☆ ☆ ☆ ☆

Prepare Ahead — WHAT I LIKED...   WHAT I WOULD CHANGE...

☐ I PACKED WHAT I PLANNED   ☐ I MADE SUBSTITUTIONS   ☐ I DIDN'T MAKE A LUNCH

Prepare Ahead — WHAT I LIKED...   WHAT I WOULD CHANGE...

☐ I PACKED WHAT I PLANNED   ☐ I MADE SUBSTITUTIONS   ☐ I DIDN'T MAKE A LUNCH

Prepare Ahead — WHAT I LIKED...   WHAT I WOULD CHANGE...

☐ I PACKED WHAT I PLANNED   ☐ I MADE SUBSTITUTIONS   ☐ I DIDN'T MAKE A LUNCH

Prepare Ahead — WHAT I LIKED...   WHAT I WOULD CHANGE...

☐ I PACKED WHAT I PLANNED   ☐ I MADE SUBSTITUTIONS   ☐ I DIDN'T MAKE A LUNCH

Grocery List

☐
☐
☐
☐
☐
☐
☐
☐
☐
☐
☐
☐
☐
☐
☐
☐
☐
☐
☐
☐
☐
☐
☐

Leftovers /
groceries that
need to be used

✂

"Part of the secret to success in life is to eat what you like and let the food fight it out inside."
– Mark Twain

Date: _____ M T W Th F S Su

DRINKS

SNACKS: _____

Recipes & Notes

RATING ☆ ☆ ☆ ☆ ☆

Date: _____ M T W Th F S Su

DRINKS

SNACKS: _____

Recipes & Notes

RATING ☆ ☆ ☆ ☆ ☆

Date: _____ M T W Th F S Su

DRINKS

SNACKS: _____

Recipes & Notes

RATING ☆ ☆ ☆ ☆ ☆

Date: _____ M T W Th F S Su

DRINKS

SNACKS: _____

Recipes & Notes

RATING ☆ ☆ ☆ ☆ ☆

Prepare Ahead —————— WHAT I LIKED...   WHAT I WOULD CHANGE...

☐
☐
☐
☐
☐
☐
☐
☐
☐ I PACKED WHAT I PLANNED   ☐ I MADE SUBSTITUTIONS   ☐ I DIDN'T MAKE A LUNCH
☐
Prepare Ahead —————— WHAT I LIKED...   WHAT I WOULD CHANGE...
☐
☐
☐
☐
☐
☐
☐
☐
☐ I PACKED WHAT I PLANNED   ☐ I MADE SUBSTITUTIONS   ☐ I DIDN'T MAKE A LUNCH
☐
Prepare Ahead —————— WHAT I LIKED...   WHAT I WOULD CHANGE...
☐
☐
☐
☐
☐
☐
☐
☐ I PACKED WHAT I PLANNED   ☐ I MADE SUBSTITUTIONS   ☐ I DIDN'T MAKE A LUNCH
☐

Prepare Ahead —————— WHAT I LIKED...   WHAT I WOULD CHANGE...

Leftovers /
groceries that
need to be used

✂

☐ I PACKED WHAT I PLANNED   ☐ I MADE SUBSTITUTIONS   ☐ I DIDN'T MAKE A LUNCH

93

"It takes 21 days. 21 days of healthy eating and working out and it will become a habit."

Date: _____ M T W Th F S Su

DRINKS

Recipes & Notes

SNACKS:

RATING ☆ ☆ ☆ ☆ ☆

Date: _____ M T W Th F S Su

DRINKS

Recipes & Notes

SNACKS:

RATING ☆ ☆ ☆ ☆ ☆

Date: _____ M T W Th F S Su

DRINKS

Recipes & Notes

SNACKS:

RATING ☆ ☆ ☆ ☆ ☆

Date: _____ M T W Th F S Su

DRINKS

Recipes & Notes

SNACKS:

RATING ☆ ☆ ☆ ☆ ☆

Prepare Ahead — WHAT I LIKED...   WHAT I WOULD CHANGE...

☐ I PACKED WHAT I PLANNED   ☐ I MADE SUBSTITUTIONS   ☐ I DIDN'T MAKE A LUNCH

Prepare Ahead — WHAT I LIKED...   WHAT I WOULD CHANGE...

☐ I PACKED WHAT I PLANNED   ☐ I MADE SUBSTITUTIONS   ☐ I DIDN'T MAKE A LUNCH

Prepare Ahead — WHAT I LIKED...   WHAT I WOULD CHANGE...

☐ I PACKED WHAT I PLANNED   ☐ I MADE SUBSTITUTIONS   ☐ I DIDN'T MAKE A LUNCH

Prepare Ahead — WHAT I LIKED...   WHAT I WOULD CHANGE...

☐ I PACKED WHAT I PLANNED   ☐ I MADE SUBSTITUTIONS   ☐ I DIDN'T MAKE A LUNCH

Grocery List

☐
☐
☐
☐
☐
☐
☐
☐
☐
☐
☐
☐
☐
☐
☐
☐
☐
☐
☐
☐
☐
☐

Leftovers /
groceries that
need to be used

✂

95

Date: _____ M T W Th F S Su

Recipes & Notes

DRINKS

SNACKS:

RATING ☆ ☆ ☆ ☆ ☆

Date: _____ M T W Th F S Su

Recipes & Notes

DRINKS

SNACKS:

RATING ☆ ☆ ☆ ☆ ☆

Date: _____ M T W Th F S Su

Recipes & Notes

DRINKS

SNACKS:

RATING ☆ ☆ ☆ ☆ ☆

Date: _____ M T W Th F S Su

Recipes & Notes

DRINKS

SNACKS:

RATING ☆ ☆ ☆ ☆ ☆

Prepare Ahead   WHAT I LIKED...   WHAT I WOULD CHANGE...

☐ I PACKED WHAT I PLANNED   ☐ I MADE SUBSTITUTIONS   ☐ I DIDN'T MAKE A LUNCH

Prepare Ahead   WHAT I LIKED...   WHAT I WOULD CHANGE...

☐ I PACKED WHAT I PLANNED   ☐ I MADE SUBSTITUTIONS   ☐ I DIDN'T MAKE A LUNCH

Prepare Ahead   WHAT I LIKED...   WHAT I WOULD CHANGE...

☐ I PACKED WHAT I PLANNED   ☐ I MADE SUBSTITUTIONS   ☐ I DIDN'T MAKE A LUNCH

Prepare Ahead   WHAT I LIKED...   WHAT I WOULD CHANGE...

☐ I PACKED WHAT I PLANNED   ☐ I MADE SUBSTITUTIONS   ☐ I DIDN'T MAKE A LUNCH

Grocery List

☐
☐
☐
☐
☐
☐
☐
☐
☐
☐
☐
☐
☐
☐
☐
☐
☐
☐
☐
☐
☐
☐
☐
☐

Leftovers /
groceries that
need to be used

"ADMIT IT. We've all hidden our favourite food from our family at least once."

Date: _____   M T W Th F S Su

Recipes & Notes

DRINKS

SNACKS:

RATING ☆ ☆ ☆ ☆ ☆

Date: _____   M T W Th F S Su

Recipes & Notes

DRINKS

SNACKS:

RATING ☆ ☆ ☆ ☆ ☆

Date: _____   M T W Th F S Su

Recipes & Notes

DRINKS

SNACKS:

RATING ☆ ☆ ☆ ☆ ☆

Date: _____   M T W Th F S Su

Recipes & Notes

DRINKS

SNACKS:

RATING ☆ ☆ ☆ ☆ ☆

Prepare Ahead WHAT I LIKED... WHAT I WOULD CHANGE...

☐ I PACKED WHAT I PLANNED ☐ I MADE SUBSTITUTIONS ☐ I DIDN'T MAKE A LUNCH

Prepare Ahead WHAT I LIKED... WHAT I WOULD CHANGE...

☐ I PACKED WHAT I PLANNED ☐ I MADE SUBSTITUTIONS ☐ I DIDN'T MAKE A LUNCH

Prepare Ahead WHAT I LIKED... WHAT I WOULD CHANGE...

☐ I PACKED WHAT I PLANNED ☐ I MADE SUBSTITUTIONS ☐ I DIDN'T MAKE A LUNCH

Prepare Ahead WHAT I LIKED... WHAT I WOULD CHANGE...

☐ I PACKED WHAT I PLANNED ☐ I MADE SUBSTITUTIONS ☐ I DIDN'T MAKE A LUNCH

Grocery List

☐
☐
☐
☐
☐
☐
☐
☐
☐
☐
☐
☐
☐
☐
☐
☐
☐
☐
☐
☐
☐
☐
☐

Leftovers / groceries that need to be used

✂

"It may look like I'm having really deep thoughts but 99% of the time I'm just thinking about what food I'm going to eat later."

Date: _____   M T W Th F S Su   *Recipes & Notes*

DRINKS

SNACKS:

RATING ☆ ☆ ☆ ☆ ☆

Date: _____   M T W Th F S Su   *Recipes & Notes*

DRINKS

SNACKS:

RATING ☆ ☆ ☆ ☆ ☆

Date: _____   M T W Th F S Su   *Recipes & Notes*

DRINKS

SNACKS:

RATING ☆ ☆ ☆ ☆ ☆

Date: _____   M T W Th F S Su   *Recipes & Notes*

DRINKS

SNACKS:

RATING ☆ ☆ ☆ ☆ ☆

Prepare Ahead —————— WHAT I LIKED...   WHAT I WOULD CHANGE... —————

☐ I PACKED WHAT I PLANNED   ☐ I MADE SUBSTITUTIONS   ☐ I DIDN'T MAKE A LUNCH

Prepare Ahead —————— WHAT I LIKED...   WHAT I WOULD CHANGE... —————

☐ I PACKED WHAT I PLANNED   ☐ I MADE SUBSTITUTIONS   ☐ I DIDN'T MAKE A LUNCH

Prepare Ahead —————— WHAT I LIKED...   WHAT I WOULD CHANGE... —————

☐ I PACKED WHAT I PLANNED   ☐ I MADE SUBSTITUTIONS   ☐ I DIDN'T MAKE A LUNCH

Prepare Ahead —————— WHAT I LIKED...   WHAT I WOULD CHANGE... —————

☐ I PACKED WHAT I PLANNED   ☐ I MADE SUBSTITUTIONS   ☐ I DIDN'T MAKE A LUNCH

Grocery List

☐
☐
☐
☐
☐
☐
☐
☐
☐
☐
☐
☐
☐
☐
☐
☐
☐
☐
☐
☐
☐
☐
☐
☐

Leftovers / groceries that need to be used

✂

"When diet is wrong, medicine is of no use. When diet is correct, medicine is of no need."
— Ayurvedic Proverb

Date: _____ M T W Th F S Su

DRINKS

SNACKS:

Recipes & Notes

RATING ☆ ☆ ☆ ☆ ☆

Date: _____ M T W Th F S Su

DRINKS

SNACKS:

Recipes & Notes

RATING ☆ ☆ ☆ ☆ ☆

Date: _____ M T W Th F S Su

DRINKS

SNACKS:

Recipes & Notes

RATING ☆ ☆ ☆ ☆ ☆

Date: _____ M T W Th F S Su

DRINKS

SNACKS:

Recipes & Notes

RATING ☆ ☆ ☆ ☆ ☆

Prepare Ahead — WHAT I LIKED...   WHAT I WOULD CHANGE...

☐ I PACKED WHAT I PLANNED   ☐ I MADE SUBSTITUTIONS   ☐ I DIDN'T MAKE A LUNCH

Prepare Ahead — WHAT I LIKED...   WHAT I WOULD CHANGE...

☐ I PACKED WHAT I PLANNED   ☐ I MADE SUBSTITUTIONS   ☐ I DIDN'T MAKE A LUNCH

Prepare Ahead — WHAT I LIKED...   WHAT I WOULD CHANGE...

☐ I PACKED WHAT I PLANNED   ☐ I MADE SUBSTITUTIONS   ☐ I DIDN'T MAKE A LUNCH

Prepare Ahead — WHAT I LIKED...   WHAT I WOULD CHANGE...

☐ I PACKED WHAT I PLANNED   ☐ I MADE SUBSTITUTIONS   ☐ I DIDN'T MAKE A LUNCH

Grocery List

☐
☐
☐
☐
☐
☐
☐
☐
☐
☐
☐
☐
☐
☐
☐
☐
☐
☐
☐
☐
☐
☐

Leftovers / groceries that need to be used

✂

103

"I only need 3 things in life: Food, WiFi, Sleep."

Date: _____ M T W Th F S Su

Recipes & Notes

DRINKS

SNACKS: _____

RATING ☆ ☆ ☆ ☆ ☆

Date: _____ M T W Th F S Su

Recipes & Notes

DRINKS

SNACKS: _____

RATING ☆ ☆ ☆ ☆ ☆

Date: _____ M T W Th F S Su

Recipes & Notes

DRINKS

SNACKS: _____

RATING ☆ ☆ ☆ ☆ ☆

Date: _____ M T W Th F S Su

Recipes & Notes

DRINKS

SNACKS: _____

RATING ☆ ☆ ☆ ☆ ☆

Prepare Ahead — WHAT I LIKED...   WHAT I WOULD CHANGE...

☐ I PACKED WHAT I PLANNED   ☐ I MADE SUBSTITUTIONS   ☐ I DIDN'T MAKE A LUNCH

Prepare Ahead — WHAT I LIKED...   WHAT I WOULD CHANGE...

☐ I PACKED WHAT I PLANNED   ☐ I MADE SUBSTITUTIONS   ☐ I DIDN'T MAKE A LUNCH

Prepare Ahead — WHAT I LIKED...   WHAT I WOULD CHANGE...

☐ I PACKED WHAT I PLANNED   ☐ I MADE SUBSTITUTIONS   ☐ I DIDN'T MAKE A LUNCH

Prepare Ahead — WHAT I LIKED...   WHAT I WOULD CHANGE...

☐ I PACKED WHAT I PLANNED   ☐ I MADE SUBSTITUTIONS   ☐ I DIDN'T MAKE A LUNCH

Grocery List

☐
☐
☐
☐
☐
☐
☐
☐
☐
☐
☐
☐
☐
☐
☐
☐
☐
☐
☐
☐
☐
☐

Leftovers /
groceries that
need to be used

✂

"Never eat more than you can lift!" – Miss Piggy

Date: _____ M T W Th F S Su

Recipes & Notes

DRINKS

SNACKS:

RATING ☆ ☆ ☆ ☆ ☆

Date: _____ M T W Th F S Su

Recipes & Notes

DRINKS

SNACKS:

RATING ☆ ☆ ☆ ☆ ☆

Date: _____ M T W Th F S Su

Recipes & Notes

DRINKS

SNACKS:

RATING ☆ ☆ ☆ ☆ ☆

Date: _____ M T W Th F S Su

Recipes & Notes

DRINKS

SNACKS:

RATING ☆ ☆ ☆ ☆ ☆

—— *Prepare Ahead* ——   WHAT I LIKED...   WHAT I WOULD CHANGE...

☐ I PACKED WHAT I PLANNED   ☐ I MADE SUBSTITUTIONS   ☐ I DIDN'T MAKE A LUNCH

—— *Prepare Ahead* ——   WHAT I LIKED...   WHAT I WOULD CHANGE...

☐ I PACKED WHAT I PLANNED   ☐ I MADE SUBSTITUTIONS   ☐ I DIDN'T MAKE A LUNCH

—— *Prepare Ahead* ——   WHAT I LIKED...   WHAT I WOULD CHANGE...

☐ I PACKED WHAT I PLANNED   ☐ I MADE SUBSTITUTIONS   ☐ I DIDN'T MAKE A LUNCH

—— *Prepare Ahead* ——   WHAT I LIKED...   WHAT I WOULD CHANGE...

☐ I PACKED WHAT I PLANNED   ☐ I MADE SUBSTITUTIONS   ☐ I DIDN'T MAKE A LUNCH

Grocery List

☐
☐
☐
☐
☐
☐
☐
☐
☐
☐
☐
☐
☐
☐
☐
☐
☐
☐
☐
☐
☐
☐
☐
☐

Leftovers /
groceries that
need to be used

✂

Date: M T W Th F S Su   *Recipes & Notes*

DRINKS

SNACKS:

RATING ☆ ☆ ☆ ☆ ☆

Date: M T W Th F S Su   *Recipes & Notes*

DRINKS

SNACKS:

RATING ☆ ☆ ☆ ☆ ☆

Date: M T W Th F S Su   *Recipes & Notes*

DRINKS

SNACKS:

RATING ☆ ☆ ☆ ☆ ☆

Date: M T W Th F S Su   *Recipes & Notes*

DRINKS

SNACKS:

RATING ☆ ☆ ☆ ☆ ☆

Prepare Ahead

WHAT I LIKED...   WHAT I WOULD CHANGE...

☐ I PACKED WHAT I PLANNED   ☐ I MADE SUBSTITUTIONS   ☐ I DIDN'T MAKE A LUNCH

Prepare Ahead

WHAT I LIKED...   WHAT I WOULD CHANGE...

☐ I PACKED WHAT I PLANNED   ☐ I MADE SUBSTITUTIONS   ☐ I DIDN'T MAKE A LUNCH

Prepare Ahead

WHAT I LIKED...   WHAT I WOULD CHANGE...

☐ I PACKED WHAT I PLANNED   ☐ I MADE SUBSTITUTIONS   ☐ I DIDN'T MAKE A LUNCH

Prepare Ahead

WHAT I LIKED...   WHAT I WOULD CHANGE...

☐ I PACKED WHAT I PLANNED   ☐ I MADE SUBSTITUTIONS   ☐ I DIDN'T MAKE A LUNCH

Grocery List

☐
☐
☐
☐
☐
☐
☐
☐
☐
☐
☐
☐
☐
☐
☐
☐
☐
☐
☐
☐
☐
☐
☐
☐

Leftovers /
groceries that
need to be used

✂

"You know that you have eaten way too much junk food when you start actually craving something healthy."

Date: _____ M T W Th F S Su

Recipes & Notes

DRINKS

SNACKS:

RATING ☆ ☆ ☆ ☆ ☆

Date: _____ M T W Th F S Su

Recipes & Notes

DRINKS

SNACKS:

RATING ☆ ☆ ☆ ☆ ☆

Date: _____ M T W Th F S Su

Recipes & Notes

DRINKS

SNACKS:

RATING ☆ ☆ ☆ ☆ ☆

Date: _____ M T W Th F S Su

Recipes & Notes

DRINKS

SNACKS:

RATING ☆ ☆ ☆ ☆ ☆

Prepare Ahead   WHAT I LIKED...   WHAT I WOULD CHANGE...   **Grocery List**

☐ I PACKED WHAT I PLANNED   ☐ I MADE SUBSTITUTIONS   ☐ I DIDN'T MAKE A LUNCH

Prepare Ahead   WHAT I LIKED...   WHAT I WOULD CHANGE...

☐ I PACKED WHAT I PLANNED   ☐ I MADE SUBSTITUTIONS   ☐ I DIDN'T MAKE A LUNCH

Prepare Ahead   WHAT I LIKED...   WHAT I WOULD CHANGE...

☐
☐
☐
☐
☐
☐
☐
☐
☐
☐
☐
☐
☐
☐
☐
☐
☐
☐
☐
☐
☐
☐
☐

☐ I PACKED WHAT I PLANNED   ☐ I MADE SUBSTITUTIONS   ☐ I DIDN'T MAKE A LUNCH

Prepare Ahead   WHAT I LIKED...   WHAT I WOULD CHANGE...   Leftovers / groceries that need to be used

✂

☐ I PACKED WHAT I PLANNED   ☐ I MADE SUBSTITUTIONS   ☐ I DIDN'T MAKE A LUNCH

111

"Back in my day. We played outside not online. Parents called our name, not our cell phone, and if you didn't eat what mum cooked you didn't eat. Yes, I know I'm old!"

Date: _____   M T W Th F S Su

Recipes & Notes

DRINKS

SNACKS:

RATING ☆ ☆ ☆ ☆ ☆

Date: _____   M T W Th F S Su

Recipes & Notes

DRINKS

SNACKS:

RATING ☆ ☆ ☆ ☆ ☆

Date: _____   M T W Th F S Su

Recipes & Notes

DRINKS

SNACKS:

RATING ☆ ☆ ☆ ☆ ☆

Date: _____   M T W Th F S Su

Recipes & Notes

DRINKS

SNACKS:

RATING ☆ ☆ ☆ ☆ ☆

Prepare Ahead ———— WHAT I LIKED...   WHAT I WOULD CHANGE...

☐ I PACKED WHAT I PLANNED   ☐ I MADE SUBSTITUTIONS   ☐ I DIDN'T MAKE A LUNCH

Prepare Ahead ———— WHAT I LIKED...   WHAT I WOULD CHANGE...

☐ I PACKED WHAT I PLANNED   ☐ I MADE SUBSTITUTIONS   ☐ I DIDN'T MAKE A LUNCH

Prepare Ahead ———— WHAT I LIKED...   WHAT I WOULD CHANGE...

☐ I PACKED WHAT I PLANNED   ☐ I MADE SUBSTITUTIONS   ☐ I DIDN'T MAKE A LUNCH

Prepare Ahead ———— WHAT I LIKED...   WHAT I WOULD CHANGE...

☐ I PACKED WHAT I PLANNED   ☐ I MADE SUBSTITUTIONS   ☐ I DIDN'T MAKE A LUNCH

Grocery List

☐
☐
☐
☐
☐
☐
☐
☐
☐
☐
☐
☐
☐
☐
☐
☐
☐
☐
☐
☐
☐
☐

Leftovers /
groceries that
need to be used

✂

Date: _____ M T W Th F S Su

DRINKS

SNACKS: _____

Recipes & Notes

_____
_____
_____
_____
_____
_____
_____

RATING ☆ ☆ ☆ ☆ ☆

Date: _____ M T W Th F S Su

DRINKS

SNACKS: _____

Recipes & Notes

_____
_____
_____
_____
_____
_____
_____

RATING ☆ ☆ ☆ ☆ ☆

Date: _____ M T W Th F S Su

DRINKS

SNACKS: _____

Recipes & Notes

_____
_____
_____
_____
_____
_____
_____

RATING ☆ ☆ ☆ ☆ ☆

Date: _____ M T W Th F S Su

DRINKS

SNACKS: _____

Recipes & Notes

_____
_____
_____
_____
_____
_____
_____

RATING ☆ ☆ ☆ ☆ ☆

Prepare Ahead — WHAT I LIKED... — WHAT I WOULD CHANGE...

☐ I PACKED WHAT I PLANNED   ☐ I MADE SUBSTITUTIONS   ☐ I DIDN'T MAKE A LUNCH

Prepare Ahead — WHAT I LIKED... — WHAT I WOULD CHANGE...

☐ I PACKED WHAT I PLANNED   ☐ I MADE SUBSTITUTIONS   ☐ I DIDN'T MAKE A LUNCH

Prepare Ahead — WHAT I LIKED... — WHAT I WOULD CHANGE...

☐ I PACKED WHAT I PLANNED   ☐ I MADE SUBSTITUTIONS   ☐ I DIDN'T MAKE A LUNCH

Prepare Ahead — WHAT I LIKED... — WHAT I WOULD CHANGE...

☐ I PACKED WHAT I PLANNED   ☐ I MADE SUBSTITUTIONS   ☐ I DIDN'T MAKE A LUNCH

Grocery List

☐
☐
☐
☐
☐
☐
☐
☐
☐
☐
☐
☐
☐
☐
☐
☐
☐
☐
☐
☐
☐
☐

Leftovers / groceries that need to be used

✂

"Han-gry: a state of anger caused by lack of food, hunger causing a negative change in emotional state."

Date: _____   M T W Th F S Su

Recipes & Notes

DRINKS

SNACKS:

RATING ☆ ☆ ☆ ☆ ☆

Date: _____   M T W Th F S Su

Recipes & Notes

DRINKS

SNACKS:

RATING ☆ ☆ ☆ ☆ ☆

Date: _____   M T W Th F S Su

Recipes & Notes

DRINKS

SNACKS:

RATING ☆ ☆ ☆ ☆ ☆

Date: _____   M T W Th F S Su

Recipes & Notes

DRINKS

SNACKS:

RATING ☆ ☆ ☆ ☆ ☆

Prepare Ahead ——— WHAT I LIKED... WHAT I WOULD CHANGE...

☐ I PACKED WHAT I PLANNED ☐ I MADE SUBSTITUTIONS ☐ I DIDN'T MAKE A LUNCH

Prepare Ahead ——— WHAT I LIKED... WHAT I WOULD CHANGE...

☐ I PACKED WHAT I PLANNED ☐ I MADE SUBSTITUTIONS ☐ I DIDN'T MAKE A LUNCH

Prepare Ahead ——— WHAT I LIKED... WHAT I WOULD CHANGE...

☐ I PACKED WHAT I PLANNED ☐ I MADE SUBSTITUTIONS ☐ I DIDN'T MAKE A LUNCH

Prepare Ahead ——— WHAT I LIKED... WHAT I WOULD CHANGE...

☐ I PACKED WHAT I PLANNED ☐ I MADE SUBSTITUTIONS ☐ I DIDN'T MAKE A LUNCH

Grocery List

☐
☐
☐
☐
☐
☐
☐
☐
☐
☐
☐
☐
☐
☐
☐
☐
☐
☐
☐
☐
☐
☐
☐

Leftovers /
groceries that
need to be used

✂

117

Date: _____ M T W Th F S Su

DRINKS

SNACKS:

Recipes & Notes

RATING ☆ ☆ ☆ ☆ ☆

Date: _____ M T W Th F S Su

DRINKS

SNACKS:

Recipes & Notes

RATING ☆ ☆ ☆ ☆ ☆

Date: _____ M T W Th F S Su

DRINKS

SNACKS:

Recipes & Notes

RATING ☆ ☆ ☆ ☆ ☆

Date: _____ M T W Th F S Su

DRINKS

SNACKS:

Recipes & Notes

RATING ☆ ☆ ☆ ☆ ☆

Prepare Ahead — WHAT I LIKED...   WHAT I WOULD CHANGE...

☐ I PACKED WHAT I PLANNED   ☐ I MADE SUBSTITUTIONS   ☐ I DIDN'T MAKE A LUNCH

Prepare Ahead — WHAT I LIKED...   WHAT I WOULD CHANGE...

☐ I PACKED WHAT I PLANNED   ☐ I MADE SUBSTITUTIONS   ☐ I DIDN'T MAKE A LUNCH

Prepare Ahead — WHAT I LIKED...   WHAT I WOULD CHANGE...

☐ I PACKED WHAT I PLANNED   ☐ I MADE SUBSTITUTIONS   ☐ I DIDN'T MAKE A LUNCH

Prepare Ahead — WHAT I LIKED...   WHAT I WOULD CHANGE...

☐ I PACKED WHAT I PLANNED   ☐ I MADE SUBSTITUTIONS   ☐ I DIDN'T MAKE A LUNCH

Grocery List

☐
☐
☐
☐
☐
☐
☐
☐
☐
☐
☐
☐
☐
☐
☐
☐
☐
☐
☐
☐
☐
☐
☐
☐

Leftovers / groceries that need to be used

119

Date: _____   M T W Th F S Su

Recipes & Notes

DRINKS

RATING ☆ ☆ ☆ ☆ ☆

SNACKS: _____

Date: _____   M T W Th F S Su

Recipes & Notes

DRINKS

SNACKS: _____

RATING ☆ ☆ ☆ ☆ ☆

Date: _____   M T W Th F S Su

Recipes & Notes

DRINKS

SNACKS: _____

RATING ☆ ☆ ☆ ☆ ☆

Date: _____   M T W Th F S Su

Recipes & Notes

DRINKS

SNACKS: _____

RATING ☆ ☆ ☆ ☆ ☆

Prepare Ahead — WHAT I LIKED... — WHAT I WOULD CHANGE...

☐ I PACKED WHAT I PLANNED   ☐ I MADE SUBSTITUTIONS   ☐ I DIDN'T MAKE A LUNCH

Prepare Ahead — WHAT I LIKED... — WHAT I WOULD CHANGE...

☐ I PACKED WHAT I PLANNED   ☐ I MADE SUBSTITUTIONS   ☐ I DIDN'T MAKE A LUNCH

Prepare Ahead — WHAT I LIKED... — WHAT I WOULD CHANGE...

☐ I PACKED WHAT I PLANNED   ☐ I MADE SUBSTITUTIONS   ☐ I DIDN'T MAKE A LUNCH

Prepare Ahead — WHAT I LIKED... — WHAT I WOULD CHANGE...

☐ I PACKED WHAT I PLANNED   ☐ I MADE SUBSTITUTIONS   ☐ I DIDN'T MAKE A LUNCH

Grocery List

☐
☐
☐
☐
☐
☐
☐
☐
☐
☐
☐
☐
☐
☐
☐
☐
☐
☐
☐
☐
☐
☐

Leftovers /
groceries that
need to be used

✂

Date: _____ M T W Th F S Su

Recipes & Notes

DRINKS

SNACKS: _____

RATING ☆ ☆ ☆ ☆ ☆

Date: _____ M T W Th F S Su

Recipes & Notes

DRINKS

SNACKS: _____

RATING ☆ ☆ ☆ ☆ ☆

Date: _____ M T W Th F S Su

Recipes & Notes

DRINKS

SNACKS: _____

RATING ☆ ☆ ☆ ☆ ☆

Date: _____ M T W Th F S Su

Recipes & Notes

DRINKS

SNACKS: _____

RATING ☆ ☆ ☆ ☆ ☆

Prepare Ahead | WHAT I LIKED... | WHAT I WOULD CHANGE...

☐ I PACKED WHAT I PLANNED   ☐ I MADE SUBSTITUTIONS   ☐ I DIDN'T MAKE A LUNCH

Prepare Ahead | WHAT I LIKED... | WHAT I WOULD CHANGE...

☐ I PACKED WHAT I PLANNED   ☐ I MADE SUBSTITUTIONS   ☐ I DIDN'T MAKE A LUNCH

Prepare Ahead | WHAT I LIKED... | WHAT I WOULD CHANGE...

☐ I PACKED WHAT I PLANNED   ☐ I MADE SUBSTITUTIONS   ☐ I DIDN'T MAKE A LUNCH

Prepare Ahead | WHAT I LIKED... | WHAT I WOULD CHANGE...

☐ I PACKED WHAT I PLANNED   ☐ I MADE SUBSTITUTIONS   ☐ I DIDN'T MAKE A LUNCH

Grocery List

☐
☐
☐
☐
☐
☐
☐
☐
☐
☐
☐
☐
☐
☐
☐
☐
☐
☐
☐
☐
☐

Leftovers / groceries that need to be used

✂

Date: _____   M   T   W   Th   F   S   Su

Recipes & Notes

DRINKS

SNACKS: _____

RATING ☆ ☆ ☆ ☆ ☆

Date: _____   M   T   W   Th   F   S   Su

Recipes & Notes

DRINKS

SNACKS: _____

RATING ☆ ☆ ☆ ☆ ☆

Date: _____   M   T   W   Th   F   S   Su

Recipes & Notes

DRINKS

SNACKS: _____

RATING ☆ ☆ ☆ ☆ ☆

Date: _____   M   T   W   Th   F   S   Su

Recipes & Notes

DRINKS

SNACKS: _____

RATING ☆ ☆ ☆ ☆ ☆

Prepare Ahead ———— WHAT I LIKED...   WHAT I WOULD CHANGE...

☐ I PACKED WHAT I PLANNED   ☐ I MADE SUBSTITUTIONS   ☐ I DIDN'T MAKE A LUNCH

Prepare Ahead ———— WHAT I LIKED...   WHAT I WOULD CHANGE...

☐ I PACKED WHAT I PLANNED   ☐ I MADE SUBSTITUTIONS   ☐ I DIDN'T MAKE A LUNCH

Prepare Ahead ———— WHAT I LIKED...   WHAT I WOULD CHANGE...

☐ I PACKED WHAT I PLANNED   ☐ I MADE SUBSTITUTIONS   ☐ I DIDN'T MAKE A LUNCH

Prepare Ahead ———— WHAT I LIKED...   WHAT I WOULD CHANGE...

☐
☐
☐
☐
☐
☐
☐
☐
☐
☐
☐
☐
☐
☐
☐
☐
☐
☐
☐
☐
☐
☐
☐
☐

Leftovers /
groceries that
need to be used

☐ I PACKED WHAT I PLANNED   ☐ I MADE SUBSTITUTIONS   ☐ I DIDN'T MAKE A LUNCH

"I'm into colourful food. Obviously lots of flavour, but I think we eat with our eyes first, so it has to look great. The presentation has to be great." – Giada De Laurentiis

Date: _____   M T W Th F S Su   *Recipes & Notes*

DRINKS

SNACKS: _____

RATING ☆ ☆ ☆ ☆ ☆

Date: _____   M T W Th F S Su   *Recipes & Notes*

DRINKS

SNACKS: _____

RATING ☆ ☆ ☆ ☆ ☆

Date: _____   M T W Th F S Su   *Recipes & Notes*

DRINKS

SNACKS: _____

RATING ☆ ☆ ☆ ☆ ☆

Date: _____   M T W Th F S Su   *Recipes & Notes*

DRINKS

SNACKS: _____

RATING ☆ ☆ ☆ ☆ ☆

Prepare Ahead ——— WHAT I LIKED...   WHAT I WOULD CHANGE...

☐ I PACKED WHAT I PLANNED   ☐ I MADE SUBSTITUTIONS   ☐ I DIDN'T MAKE A LUNCH

Prepare Ahead ——— WHAT I LIKED...   WHAT I WOULD CHANGE...

☐ I PACKED WHAT I PLANNED   ☐ I MADE SUBSTITUTIONS   ☐ I DIDN'T MAKE A LUNCH

Prepare Ahead ——— WHAT I LIKED...   WHAT I WOULD CHANGE...

☐ I PACKED WHAT I PLANNED   ☐ I MADE SUBSTITUTIONS   ☐ I DIDN'T MAKE A LUNCH

Prepare Ahead ——— WHAT I LIKED...   WHAT I WOULD CHANGE...

☐ I PACKED WHAT I PLANNED   ☐ I MADE SUBSTITUTIONS   ☐ I DIDN'T MAKE A LUNCH

Grocery List

☐
☐
☐
☐
☐
☐
☐
☐
☐
☐
☐
☐
☐
☐
☐
☐
☐
☐
☐
☐
☐
☐
☐
☐

Leftovers /
groceries that
need to be used

✂

127

"Think of food as fuel – embrace food, and know that it is there to feed us, not control us or harm us. You mustn't be scared of food." – Cassey Ho

Date: _____ M T W Th F S Su

Recipes & Notes

DRINKS

SNACKS:

RATING ☆ ☆ ☆ ☆ ☆

Date: _____ M T W Th F S Su

Recipes & Notes

DRINKS

SNACKS:

RATING ☆ ☆ ☆ ☆ ☆

Date: _____ M T W Th F S Su

Recipes & Notes

DRINKS

SNACKS:

RATING ☆ ☆ ☆ ☆ ☆

Date: _____ M T W Th F S Su

Recipes & Notes

DRINKS

SNACKS:

RATING ☆ ☆ ☆ ☆ ☆

Prepare Ahead WHAT I LIKED... WHAT I WOULD CHANGE...

☐ I PACKED WHAT I PLANNED ☐ I MADE SUBSTITUTIONS ☐ I DIDN'T MAKE A LUNCH

Prepare Ahead WHAT I LIKED... WHAT I WOULD CHANGE...

☐ I PACKED WHAT I PLANNED ☐ I MADE SUBSTITUTIONS ☐ I DIDN'T MAKE A LUNCH

Prepare Ahead WHAT I LIKED... WHAT I WOULD CHANGE...

☐ I PACKED WHAT I PLANNED ☐ I MADE SUBSTITUTIONS ☐ I DIDN'T MAKE A LUNCH

Prepare Ahead WHAT I LIKED... WHAT I WOULD CHANGE...

☐ I PACKED WHAT I PLANNED ☐ I MADE SUBSTITUTIONS ☐ I DIDN'T MAKE A LUNCH

Grocery List

☐
☐
☐
☐
☐
☐
☐
☐
☐
☐
☐
☐
☐
☐
☐
☐
☐
☐
☐
☐
☐
☐

Leftovers / groceries that need to be used

✂

"It's not how much you eat, it's what you eat."

Date: _____ M T W Th F S Su

Recipes & Notes

DRINKS

SNACKS:

RATING ☆ ☆ ☆ ☆ ☆

Date: _____ M T W Th F S Su

Recipes & Notes

DRINKS

SNACKS:

RATING ☆ ☆ ☆ ☆ ☆

Date: _____ M T W Th F S Su

Recipes & Notes

DRINKS

SNACKS:

RATING ☆ ☆ ☆ ☆ ☆

Date: _____ M T W Th F S Su

Recipes & Notes

DRINKS

SNACKS:

RATING ☆ ☆ ☆ ☆ ☆

Prepare Ahead   WHAT I LIKED...   WHAT I WOULD CHANGE...

☐ I PACKED WHAT I PLANNED   ☐ I MADE SUBSTITUTIONS   ☐ I DIDN'T MAKE A LUNCH

Prepare Ahead   WHAT I LIKED...   WHAT I WOULD CHANGE...

☐ I PACKED WHAT I PLANNED   ☐ I MADE SUBSTITUTIONS   ☐ I DIDN'T MAKE A LUNCH

Prepare Ahead   WHAT I LIKED...   WHAT I WOULD CHANGE...

☐ I PACKED WHAT I PLANNED   ☐ I MADE SUBSTITUTIONS   ☐ I DIDN'T MAKE A LUNCH

Prepare Ahead   WHAT I LIKED...   WHAT I WOULD CHANGE...

☐ I PACKED WHAT I PLANNED   ☐ I MADE SUBSTITUTIONS   ☐ I DIDN'T MAKE A LUNCH

Grocery List

☐
☐
☐
☐
☐
☐
☐
☐
☐
☐
☐
☐
☐
☐
☐
☐
☐
☐
☐
☐
☐
☐
☐

Leftovers / groceries that need to be used

131

Date: _____   M   T   W   Th   F   S   Su

Recipes & Notes

DRINKS

SNACKS:

RATING ☆ ☆ ☆ ☆ ☆

Date: _____   M   T   W   Th   F   S   Su

Recipes & Notes

DRINKS

SNACKS:

RATING ☆ ☆ ☆ ☆ ☆

Date: _____   M   T   W   Th   F   S   Su

Recipes & Notes

DRINKS

SNACKS:

RATING ☆ ☆ ☆ ☆ ☆

Date: _____   M   T   W   Th   F   S   Su

Recipes & Notes

DRINKS

SNACKS:

RATING ☆ ☆ ☆ ☆ ☆

Prepare Ahead ———————— WHAT I LIKED...   WHAT I WOULD CHANGE...

☐ I PACKED WHAT I PLANNED   ☐ I MADE SUBSTITUTIONS   ☐ I DIDN'T MAKE A LUNCH

Prepare Ahead ———————— WHAT I LIKED...   WHAT I WOULD CHANGE...

☐ I PACKED WHAT I PLANNED   ☐ I MADE SUBSTITUTIONS   ☐ I DIDN'T MAKE A LUNCH

Prepare Ahead ———————— WHAT I LIKED...   WHAT I WOULD CHANGE...

☐ I PACKED WHAT I PLANNED   ☐ I MADE SUBSTITUTIONS   ☐ I DIDN'T MAKE A LUNCH

Prepare Ahead ———————— WHAT I LIKED...   WHAT I WOULD CHANGE...

☐ I PACKED WHAT I PLANNED   ☐ I MADE SUBSTITUTIONS   ☐ I DIDN'T MAKE A LUNCH

Grocery List

☐
☐
☐
☐
☐
☐
☐
☐
☐
☐
☐
☐
☐
☐
☐
☐
☐
☐
☐
☐
☐
☐

Leftovers / groceries that need to be used

✂

"Our mission is to empower, educate and inspire as many people as possible to love & enjoy good food!" – Jamie Oliver

Date: _____ M T W Th F S Su

Recipes & Notes

DRINKS

SNACKS:

RATING ☆ ☆ ☆ ☆ ☆

Date: _____ M T W Th F S Su

Recipes & Notes

DRINKS

SNACKS:

RATING ☆ ☆ ☆ ☆ ☆

Date: _____ M T W Th F S Su

Recipes & Notes

DRINKS

SNACKS:

RATING ☆ ☆ ☆ ☆ ☆

Date: _____ M T W Th F S Su

Recipes & Notes

DRINKS

SNACKS:

RATING ☆ ☆ ☆ ☆ ☆

Prepare Ahead — WHAT I LIKED... — WHAT I WOULD CHANGE...

☐ I PACKED WHAT I PLANNED   ☐ I MADE SUBSTITUTIONS   ☐ I DIDN'T MAKE A LUNCH

Prepare Ahead — WHAT I LIKED... — WHAT I WOULD CHANGE...

☐ I PACKED WHAT I PLANNED   ☐ I MADE SUBSTITUTIONS   ☐ I DIDN'T MAKE A LUNCH

Prepare Ahead — WHAT I LIKED... — WHAT I WOULD CHANGE...

☐ I PACKED WHAT I PLANNED   ☐ I MADE SUBSTITUTIONS   ☐ I DIDN'T MAKE A LUNCH

Prepare Ahead — WHAT I LIKED... — WHAT I WOULD CHANGE...

☐ I PACKED WHAT I PLANNED   ☐ I MADE SUBSTITUTIONS   ☐ I DIDN'T MAKE A LUNCH

Grocery List

☐
☐
☐
☐
☐
☐
☐
☐
☐
☐
☐
☐
☐
☐
☐
☐
☐
☐
☐
☐
☐
☐
☐
☐
☐

Leftovers /
groceries that
need to be used

✂

"The trouble with eating Italian food is that five or six days later you're hungry again."

– George Miller

Date: _____   M T W Th F S Su

DRINKS

SNACKS:

RATING ☆ ☆ ☆ ☆ ☆

Recipes & Notes
_____
_____
_____
_____
_____
_____
_____

Date: _____   M T W Th F S Su

DRINKS

SNACKS:

RATING ☆ ☆ ☆ ☆ ☆

Recipes & Notes
_____
_____
_____
_____
_____
_____
_____

Date: _____   M T W Th F S Su

DRINKS

SNACKS:

RATING ☆ ☆ ☆ ☆ ☆

Recipes & Notes
_____
_____
_____
_____
_____
_____
_____

Date: _____   M T W Th F S Su

DRINKS

SNACKS:

RATING ☆ ☆ ☆ ☆ ☆

Recipes & Notes
_____
_____
_____
_____
_____
_____
_____

Prepare Ahead —————— WHAT I LIKED...   WHAT I WOULD CHANGE...

☐ I PACKED WHAT I PLANNED   ☐ I MADE SUBSTITUTIONS   ☐ I DIDN'T MAKE A LUNCH

Prepare Ahead —————— WHAT I LIKED...   WHAT I WOULD CHANGE...

☐ I PACKED WHAT I PLANNED   ☐ I MADE SUBSTITUTIONS   ☐ I DIDN'T MAKE A LUNCH

Prepare Ahead —————— WHAT I LIKED...   WHAT I WOULD CHANGE...

☐ I PACKED WHAT I PLANNED   ☐ I MADE SUBSTITUTIONS   ☐ I DIDN'T MAKE A LUNCH

Prepare Ahead —————— WHAT I LIKED...   WHAT I WOULD CHANGE...

☐ I PACKED WHAT I PLANNED   ☐ I MADE SUBSTITUTIONS   ☐ I DIDN'T MAKE A LUNCH

Grocery List

☐
☐
☐
☐
☐
☐
☐
☐
☐
☐
☐
☐
☐
☐
☐
☐
☐
☐
☐
☐
☐
☐
☐
☐
☐

Leftovers /
groceries that
need to be used

"I followed my heart and it led me into the fridge."

Date: _____   M T W Th F S Su

Recipes & Notes

SNACKS: _____

DRINKS

RATING ☆ ☆ ☆ ☆ ☆

Date: _____   M T W Th F S Su

Recipes & Notes

SNACKS: _____

DRINKS

RATING ☆ ☆ ☆ ☆ ☆

Date: _____   M T W Th F S Su

Recipes & Notes

SNACKS: _____

DRINKS

RATING ☆ ☆ ☆ ☆ ☆

Date: _____   M T W Th F S Su

Recipes & Notes

SNACKS: _____

DRINKS

RATING ☆ ☆ ☆ ☆ ☆

Prepare Ahead — WHAT I LIKED...   WHAT I WOULD CHANGE...

☐ I PACKED WHAT I PLANNED   ☐ I MADE SUBSTITUTIONS   ☐ I DIDN'T MAKE A LUNCH

Prepare Ahead — WHAT I LIKED...   WHAT I WOULD CHANGE...

☐ I PACKED WHAT I PLANNED   ☐ I MADE SUBSTITUTIONS   ☐ I DIDN'T MAKE A LUNCH

Prepare Ahead — WHAT I LIKED...   WHAT I WOULD CHANGE...

☐ I PACKED WHAT I PLANNED   ☐ I MADE SUBSTITUTIONS   ☐ I DIDN'T MAKE A LUNCH

Prepare Ahead — WHAT I LIKED...   WHAT I WOULD CHANGE...

☐ I PACKED WHAT I PLANNED   ☐ I MADE SUBSTITUTIONS   ☐ I DIDN'T MAKE A LUNCH

Grocery List

☐
☐
☐
☐
☐
☐
☐
☐
☐
☐
☐
☐
☐
☐
☐
☐
☐
☐
☐
☐
☐
☐
☐

Leftovers / groceries that need to be used

"I was going to tell you a joke about pizza. But never mind, it's too cheesy."

Date: _____ M T W Th F S Su

Recipes & Notes

DRINKS

SNACKS:

RATING ☆ ☆ ☆ ☆ ☆

Date: _____ M T W Th F S Su

Recipes & Notes

DRINKS

SNACKS:

RATING ☆ ☆ ☆ ☆ ☆

Date: _____ M T W Th F S Su

Recipes & Notes

DRINKS

SNACKS:

RATING ☆ ☆ ☆ ☆ ☆

Date: _____ M T W Th F S Su

Recipes & Notes

DRINKS

SNACKS:

RATING ☆ ☆ ☆ ☆ ☆

Prepare Ahead — WHAT I LIKED... WHAT I WOULD CHANGE...

☐ I PACKED WHAT I PLANNED   ☐ I MADE SUBSTITUTIONS   ☐ I DIDN'T MAKE A LUNCH

Prepare Ahead — WHAT I LIKED... WHAT I WOULD CHANGE...

☐ I PACKED WHAT I PLANNED   ☐ I MADE SUBSTITUTIONS   ☐ I DIDN'T MAKE A LUNCH

Prepare Ahead — WHAT I LIKED... WHAT I WOULD CHANGE...

☐ I PACKED WHAT I PLANNED   ☐ I MADE SUBSTITUTIONS   ☐ I DIDN'T MAKE A LUNCH

Prepare Ahead — WHAT I LIKED... WHAT I WOULD CHANGE...

☐ I PACKED WHAT I PLANNED   ☐ I MADE SUBSTITUTIONS   ☐ I DIDN'T MAKE A LUNCH

Grocery List

☐
☐
☐
☐
☐
☐
☐
☐
☐
☐
☐
☐
☐
☐
☐
☐
☐
☐
☐
☐
☐
☐
☐
☐

Leftovers / groceries that need to be used

141

"I won't be impressed with technology until I can download food."

Date: _____ M T W Th F S Su

Recipes & Notes

DRINKS

SNACKS:

RATING ☆ ☆ ☆ ☆ ☆

Date: _____ M T W Th F S Su

Recipes & Notes

DRINKS

SNACKS:

RATING ☆ ☆ ☆ ☆ ☆

Date: _____ M T W Th F S Su

Recipes & Notes

DRINKS

SNACKS:

RATING ☆ ☆ ☆ ☆ ☆

Date: _____ M T W Th F S Su

Recipes & Notes

DRINKS

SNACKS:

RATING ☆ ☆ ☆ ☆ ☆

Prepare Ahead — WHAT I LIKED...   WHAT I WOULD CHANGE...

☐ I PACKED WHAT I PLANNED   ☐ I MADE SUBSTITUTIONS   ☐ I DIDN'T MAKE A LUNCH

Prepare Ahead — WHAT I LIKED...   WHAT I WOULD CHANGE...

☐ I PACKED WHAT I PLANNED   ☐ I MADE SUBSTITUTIONS   ☐ I DIDN'T MAKE A LUNCH

Prepare Ahead — WHAT I LIKED...   WHAT I WOULD CHANGE...

☐ I PACKED WHAT I PLANNED   ☐ I MADE SUBSTITUTIONS   ☐ I DIDN'T MAKE A LUNCH

Prepare Ahead — WHAT I LIKED...   WHAT I WOULD CHANGE...

☐ I PACKED WHAT I PLANNED   ☐ I MADE SUBSTITUTIONS   ☐ I DIDN'T MAKE A LUNCH

Grocery List

☐
☐
☐
☐
☐
☐
☐
☐
☐
☐
☐
☐
☐
☐
☐
☐
☐
☐
☐
☐
☐
☐
☐

Leftovers /
groceries that
need to be used

143

"Well the fridge broke, so I had to eat everything." – Joey Tribbiani

Date: M T W Th F S Su

DRINKS

Recipes & Notes

SNACKS:

RATING ☆ ☆ ☆ ☆ ☆

Date: M T W Th F S Su

DRINKS

Recipes & Notes

SNACKS:

RATING ☆ ☆ ☆ ☆ ☆

Date: M T W Th F S Su

DRINKS

Recipes & Notes

SNACKS:

RATING ☆ ☆ ☆ ☆ ☆

Date: M T W Th F S Su

DRINKS

Recipes & Notes

SNACKS:

RATING ☆ ☆ ☆ ☆ ☆

—— *Prepare Ahead* —— WHAT I LIKED...   WHAT I WOULD CHANGE...

☐ I PACKED WHAT I PLANNED   ☐ I MADE SUBSTITUTIONS   ☐ I DIDN'T MAKE A LUNCH

—— *Prepare Ahead* —— WHAT I LIKED...   WHAT I WOULD CHANGE...

☐ I PACKED WHAT I PLANNED   ☐ I MADE SUBSTITUTIONS   ☐ I DIDN'T MAKE A LUNCH

—— *Prepare Ahead* —— WHAT I LIKED...   WHAT I WOULD CHANGE...

☐ I PACKED WHAT I PLANNED   ☐ I MADE SUBSTITUTIONS   ☐ I DIDN'T MAKE A LUNCH

—— *Prepare Ahead* —— WHAT I LIKED...   WHAT I WOULD CHANGE...

☐ I PACKED WHAT I PLANNED   ☐ I MADE SUBSTITUTIONS   ☐ I DIDN'T MAKE A LUNCH

Grocery List

☐
☐
☐
☐
☐
☐
☐
☐
☐
☐
☐
☐
☐
☐
☐
☐
☐
☐
☐
☐
☐
☐

Leftovers / groceries that need to be used

145

"My head says gym, but my heart says tacos!"

Date: _____ M T W Th F S Su

Recipes & Notes

DRINKS

SNACKS: _____

RATING ☆ ☆ ☆ ☆ ☆

Date: _____ M T W Th F S Su

Recipes & Notes

DRINKS

SNACKS: _____

RATING ☆ ☆ ☆ ☆ ☆

Date: _____ M T W Th F S Su

Recipes & Notes

DRINKS

SNACKS: _____

RATING ☆ ☆ ☆ ☆ ☆

Date: _____ M T W Th F S Su

Recipes & Notes

DRINKS

SNACKS: _____

RATING ☆ ☆ ☆ ☆ ☆

Prepare Ahead — WHAT I LIKED...   WHAT I WOULD CHANGE...

☐ I PACKED WHAT I PLANNED   ☐ I MADE SUBSTITUTIONS   ☐ I DIDN'T MAKE A LUNCH

Prepare Ahead — WHAT I LIKED...   WHAT I WOULD CHANGE...

☐ I PACKED WHAT I PLANNED   ☐ I MADE SUBSTITUTIONS   ☐ I DIDN'T MAKE A LUNCH

Prepare Ahead — WHAT I LIKED...   WHAT I WOULD CHANGE...

☐ I PACKED WHAT I PLANNED   ☐ I MADE SUBSTITUTIONS   ☐ I DIDN'T MAKE A LUNCH

Prepare Ahead — WHAT I LIKED...   WHAT I WOULD CHANGE...

☐ I PACKED WHAT I PLANNED   ☐ I MADE SUBSTITUTIONS   ☐ I DIDN'T MAKE A LUNCH

Grocery List

☐
☐
☐
☐
☐
☐
☐
☐
☐
☐
☐
☐
☐
☐
☐
☐
☐
☐
☐
☐
☐
☐
☐
☐

Leftovers /
groceries that
need to be used

✂

"Accidentally went grocery shopping on an empty stomach and now I'm the proud owner of aisle 5."

Date: _____   M   T   W   Th   F   S   Su

Recipes & Notes

DRINKS

SNACKS:

RATING ☆ ☆ ☆ ☆ ☆

Date: _____   M   T   W   Th   F   S   Su

Recipes & Notes

DRINKS

SNACKS:

RATING ☆ ☆ ☆ ☆ ☆

Date: _____   M   T   W   Th   F   S   Su

Recipes & Notes

DRINKS

SNACKS:

RATING ☆ ☆ ☆ ☆ ☆

Date: _____   M   T   W   Th   F   S   Su

Recipes & Notes

DRINKS

SNACKS:

RATING ☆ ☆ ☆ ☆ ☆

Prepare Ahead WHAT I LIKED... WHAT I WOULD CHANGE...

☐ I PACKED WHAT I PLANNED   ☐ I MADE SUBSTITUTIONS   ☐ I DIDN'T MAKE A LUNCH

Prepare Ahead WHAT I LIKED... WHAT I WOULD CHANGE...

☐ I PACKED WHAT I PLANNED   ☐ I MADE SUBSTITUTIONS   ☐ I DIDN'T MAKE A LUNCH

Prepare Ahead WHAT I LIKED... WHAT I WOULD CHANGE...

☐ I PACKED WHAT I PLANNED   ☐ I MADE SUBSTITUTIONS   ☐ I DIDN'T MAKE A LUNCH

Prepare Ahead WHAT I LIKED... WHAT I WOULD CHANGE...

☐ I PACKED WHAT I PLANNED   ☐ I MADE SUBSTITUTIONS   ☐ I DIDN'T MAKE A LUNCH

Grocery List

☐
☐
☐
☐
☐
☐
☐
☐
☐
☐
☐
☐
☐
☐
☐
☐
☐
☐
☐
☐
☐
☐
☐
☐

Leftovers /
groceries that
need to be used

✂

Date: _____ M T W Th F S Su

DRINKS

SNACKS: _____

Recipes & Notes

RATING ☆ ☆ ☆ ☆ ☆

Date: _____ M T W Th F S Su

DRINKS

SNACKS: _____

Recipes & Notes

RATING ☆ ☆ ☆ ☆ ☆

Date: _____ M T W Th F S Su

DRINKS

SNACKS: _____

Recipes & Notes

RATING ☆ ☆ ☆ ☆ ☆

Date: _____ M T W Th F S Su

DRINKS

SNACKS: _____

Recipes & Notes

RATING ☆ ☆ ☆ ☆ ☆

Prepare Ahead — WHAT I LIKED... WHAT I WOULD CHANGE...

☐ I PACKED WHAT I PLANNED ☐ I MADE SUBSTITUTIONS ☐ I DIDN'T MAKE A LUNCH

Prepare Ahead — WHAT I LIKED... WHAT I WOULD CHANGE...

☐ I PACKED WHAT I PLANNED ☐ I MADE SUBSTITUTIONS ☐ I DIDN'T MAKE A LUNCH

Prepare Ahead — WHAT I LIKED... WHAT I WOULD CHANGE...

☐ I PACKED WHAT I PLANNED ☐ I MADE SUBSTITUTIONS ☐ I DIDN'T MAKE A LUNCH

Prepare Ahead — WHAT I LIKED... WHAT I WOULD CHANGE...

☐ I PACKED WHAT I PLANNED ☐ I MADE SUBSTITUTIONS ☐ I DIDN'T MAKE A LUNCH

Grocery List

☐
☐
☐
☐
☐
☐
☐
☐
☐
☐
☐
☐
☐
☐
☐
☐
☐
☐
☐
☐
☐
☐
☐
☐

Leftovers /
groceries that
need to be used

Date: _____ M T W Th F S Su

Recipes & Notes

DRINKS

SNACKS:

RATING ☆ ☆ ☆ ☆ ☆

Date: _____ M T W Th F S Su

Recipes & Notes

DRINKS

SNACKS:

RATING ☆ ☆ ☆ ☆ ☆

Date: _____ M T W Th F S Su

Recipes & Notes

DRINKS

SNACKS:

RATING ☆ ☆ ☆ ☆ ☆

Date: _____ M T W Th F S Su

Recipes & Notes

DRINKS

SNACKS:

RATING ☆ ☆ ☆ ☆ ☆

Prepare Ahead — WHAT I LIKED...   WHAT I WOULD CHANGE...

☐ I PACKED WHAT I PLANNED   ☐ I MADE SUBSTITUTIONS   ☐ I DIDN'T MAKE A LUNCH

Prepare Ahead — WHAT I LIKED...   WHAT I WOULD CHANGE...

☐ I PACKED WHAT I PLANNED   ☐ I MADE SUBSTITUTIONS   ☐ I DIDN'T MAKE A LUNCH

Prepare Ahead — WHAT I LIKED...   WHAT I WOULD CHANGE...

☐ I PACKED WHAT I PLANNED   ☐ I MADE SUBSTITUTIONS   ☐ I DIDN'T MAKE A LUNCH

Prepare Ahead — WHAT I LIKED...   WHAT I WOULD CHANGE...

☐ I PACKED WHAT I PLANNED   ☐ I MADE SUBSTITUTIONS   ☐ I DIDN'T MAKE A LUNCH

Grocery List

☐
☐
☐
☐
☐
☐
☐
☐
☐
☐
☐
☐
☐
☐
☐
☐
☐
☐
☐
☐
☐
☐
☐

Leftovers / groceries that need to be used

✂

153

"All the food that is put into the stomach that the system cannot derive benefit from, is a burden to nature in her work." – Ellen G. White

Date: _____ M T W Th F S Su

DRINKS

Recipes & Notes
_____
_____
_____
_____
_____
_____

SNACKS:

RATING ☆ ☆ ☆ ☆ ☆

Date: _____ M T W Th F S Su

DRINKS

Recipes & Notes
_____
_____
_____
_____
_____
_____

SNACKS:

RATING ☆ ☆ ☆ ☆ ☆

Date: _____ M T W Th F S Su

DRINKS

Recipes & Notes
_____
_____
_____
_____
_____
_____

SNACKS:

RATING ☆ ☆ ☆ ☆ ☆

Date: _____ M T W Th F S Su

DRINKS

Recipes & Notes
_____
_____
_____
_____
_____
_____

SNACKS:

RATING ☆ ☆ ☆ ☆ ☆

Prepare Ahead   WHAT I LIKED...   WHAT I WOULD CHANGE...

☐ I PACKED WHAT I PLANNED   ☐ I MADE SUBSTITUTIONS   ☐ I DIDN'T MAKE A LUNCH

Prepare Ahead   WHAT I LIKED...   WHAT I WOULD CHANGE...

☐ I PACKED WHAT I PLANNED   ☐ I MADE SUBSTITUTIONS   ☐ I DIDN'T MAKE A LUNCH

Prepare Ahead   WHAT I LIKED...   WHAT I WOULD CHANGE...

☐ I PACKED WHAT I PLANNED   ☐ I MADE SUBSTITUTIONS   ☐ I DIDN'T MAKE A LUNCH

Prepare Ahead   WHAT I LIKED...   WHAT I WOULD CHANGE...

☐ I PACKED WHAT I PLANNED   ☐ I MADE SUBSTITUTIONS   ☐ I DIDN'T MAKE A LUNCH

Grocery List

☐
☐
☐
☐
☐
☐
☐
☐
☐
☐
☐
☐
☐
☐
☐
☐
☐
☐
☐
☐
☐
☐
☐
☐
☐
☐

Leftovers /
groceries that
need to be used

✂

"I love food so much, all I have to do is look at it and I gain 5 pounds."
- Kelly Rowland

Date: _____ M T W Th F S Su

DRINKS

SNACKS:

RATING ☆ ☆ ☆ ☆ ☆

Date: _____ M T W Th F S Su

DRINKS

SNACKS:

RATING ☆ ☆ ☆ ☆ ☆

Date: _____ M T W Th F S Su

DRINKS

SNACKS:

RATING ☆ ☆ ☆ ☆ ☆

Date: _____ M T W Th F S Su

DRINKS

SNACKS:

RATING ☆ ☆ ☆ ☆ ☆

Prepare Ahead — WHAT I LIKED...   WHAT I WOULD CHANGE...

☐ I PACKED WHAT I PLANNED   ☐ I MADE SUBSTITUTIONS   ☐ I DIDN'T MAKE A LUNCH

Prepare Ahead — WHAT I LIKED...   WHAT I WOULD CHANGE...

☐
☐
☐
☐
☐
☐
☐
☐
☐
☐
☐
☐
☐
☐

☐ I PACKED WHAT I PLANNED   ☐ I MADE SUBSTITUTIONS   ☐ I DIDN'T MAKE A LUNCH

Prepare Ahead — WHAT I LIKED...   WHAT I WOULD CHANGE...

☐
☐
☐
☐
☐
☐
☐
☐

☐ I PACKED WHAT I PLANNED   ☐ I MADE SUBSTITUTIONS   ☐ I DIDN'T MAKE A LUNCH

Prepare Ahead — WHAT I LIKED...   WHAT I WOULD CHANGE...

Leftovers /
groceries that
need to be used

✂

☐ I PACKED WHAT I PLANNED   ☐ I MADE SUBSTITUTIONS   ☐ I DIDN'T MAKE A LUNCH

Date: _____ M T W Th F S Su

Recipes & Notes

DRINKS

SNACKS: _____

RATING ☆ ☆ ☆ ☆ ☆

Date: _____ M T W Th F S Su

Recipes & Notes

DRINKS

SNACKS: _____

RATING ☆ ☆ ☆ ☆ ☆

Date: _____ M T W Th F S Su

Recipes & Notes

DRINKS

SNACKS: _____

RATING ☆ ☆ ☆ ☆ ☆

Date: _____ M T W Th F S Su

Recipes & Notes

DRINKS

SNACKS: _____

RATING ☆ ☆ ☆ ☆ ☆

Prepare Ahead ——— WHAT I LIKED...   WHAT I WOULD CHANGE...

☐ I PACKED WHAT I PLANNED   ☐ I MADE SUBSTITUTIONS   ☐ I DIDN'T MAKE A LUNCH

Prepare Ahead ——— WHAT I LIKED...   WHAT I WOULD CHANGE...

☐ I PACKED WHAT I PLANNED   ☐ I MADE SUBSTITUTIONS   ☐ I DIDN'T MAKE A LUNCH

Prepare Ahead ——— WHAT I LIKED...   WHAT I WOULD CHANGE...

☐ I PACKED WHAT I PLANNED   ☐ I MADE SUBSTITUTIONS   ☐ I DIDN'T MAKE A LUNCH

Prepare Ahead ——— WHAT I LIKED...   WHAT I WOULD CHANGE...

☐ I PACKED WHAT I PLANNED   ☐ I MADE SUBSTITUTIONS   ☐ I DIDN'T MAKE A LUNCH

Grocery List

☐
☐
☐
☐
☐
☐
☐
☐
☐
☐
☐
☐
☐
☐
☐
☐
☐
☐
☐
☐
☐
☐
☐
☐

Leftovers /
groceries that
need to be used

✂

Date: _____   M T W Th F S Su

Recipes & Notes

DRINKS

SNACKS:

RATING ☆ ☆ ☆ ☆ ☆

Date: _____   M T W Th F S Su

Recipes & Notes

DRINKS

SNACKS:

RATING ☆ ☆ ☆ ☆ ☆

Date: _____   M T W Th F S Su

Recipes & Notes

DRINKS

SNACKS:

RATING ☆ ☆ ☆ ☆ ☆

Date: _____   M T W Th F S Su

Recipes & Notes

DRINKS

SNACKS:

RATING ☆ ☆ ☆ ☆ ☆

Prepare Ahead —————— WHAT I LIKED...   WHAT I WOULD CHANGE...

☐
☐
☐
☐
☐
☐
☐ I PACKED WHAT I PLANNED   ☐ I MADE SUBSTITUTIONS   ☐ I DIDN'T MAKE A LUNCH

Prepare Ahead —————— WHAT I LIKED...   WHAT I WOULD CHANGE...

☐
☐
☐
☐
☐
☐
☐
☐ I PACKED WHAT I PLANNED   ☐ I MADE SUBSTITUTIONS   ☐ I DIDN'T MAKE A LUNCH

Prepare Ahead —————— WHAT I LIKED...   WHAT I WOULD CHANGE...

☐
☐
☐
☐
☐
☐
☐ I PACKED WHAT I PLANNED   ☐ I MADE SUBSTITUTIONS   ☐ I DIDN'T MAKE A LUNCH

Prepare Ahead —————— WHAT I LIKED...   WHAT I WOULD CHANGE...

Leftovers /
groceries that
need to be used

☐ I PACKED WHAT I PLANNED   ☐ I MADE SUBSTITUTIONS   ☐ I DIDN'T MAKE A LUNCH

163

"It's okay to play with your food." – Emeril Lagasse

Date: _____   M T W Th F S Su

DRINKS

SNACKS:

Recipes & Notes

RATING ☆ ☆ ☆ ☆ ☆

Date: _____   M T W Th F S Su

DRINKS

SNACKS:

Recipes & Notes

RATING ☆ ☆ ☆ ☆ ☆

Date: _____   M T W Th F S Su

DRINKS

SNACKS:

Recipes & Notes

RATING ☆ ☆ ☆ ☆ ☆

Date: _____   M T W Th F S Su

DRINKS

SNACKS:

Recipes & Notes

RATING ☆ ☆ ☆ ☆ ☆

--- *Prepare Ahead* --- WHAT I LIKED... WHAT I WOULD CHANGE...

☐ I PACKED WHAT I PLANNED ☐ I MADE SUBSTITUTIONS ☐ I DIDN'T MAKE A LUNCH

--- *Prepare Ahead* --- WHAT I LIKED... WHAT I WOULD CHANGE...

☐ I PACKED WHAT I PLANNED ☐ I MADE SUBSTITUTIONS ☐ I DIDN'T MAKE A LUNCH

--- *Prepare Ahead* --- WHAT I LIKED... WHAT I WOULD CHANGE...

☐ I PACKED WHAT I PLANNED ☐ I MADE SUBSTITUTIONS ☐ I DIDN'T MAKE A LUNCH

--- *Prepare Ahead* --- WHAT I LIKED... WHAT I WOULD CHANGE...

☐ I PACKED WHAT I PLANNED ☐ I MADE SUBSTITUTIONS ☐ I DIDN'T MAKE A LUNCH

Grocery List

☐
☐
☐
☐
☐
☐
☐
☐
☐
☐
☐
☐
☐
☐
☐
☐
☐
☐
☐
☐
☐
☐
☐
☐

Leftovers /
groceries that
need to be used

✂

"My mother's menu consisted of two choices: take it or leave it." – Buddy Hackett

Date: M T W Th F S Su   *Recipes & Notes*

DRINKS

SNACKS:

RATING ☆ ☆ ☆ ☆ ☆

Date: M T W Th F S Su   *Recipes & Notes*

DRINKS

SNACKS:

RATING ☆ ☆ ☆ ☆ ☆

Date: M T W Th F S Su   *Recipes & Notes*

DRINKS

SNACKS:

RATING ☆ ☆ ☆ ☆ ☆

Date: M T W Th F S Su   *Recipes & Notes*

DRINKS

SNACKS:

RATING ☆ ☆ ☆ ☆ ☆

— *Prepare Ahead* — WHAT I LIKED... WHAT I WOULD CHANGE...

☐ I PACKED WHAT I PLANNED ☐ I MADE SUBSTITUTIONS ☐ I DIDN'T MAKE A LUNCH

— *Prepare Ahead* — WHAT I LIKED... WHAT I WOULD CHANGE...

☐ I PACKED WHAT I PLANNED ☐ I MADE SUBSTITUTIONS ☐ I DIDN'T MAKE A LUNCH

— *Prepare Ahead* — WHAT I LIKED... WHAT I WOULD CHANGE...

☐ I PACKED WHAT I PLANNED ☐ I MADE SUBSTITUTIONS ☐ I DIDN'T MAKE A LUNCH

— *Prepare Ahead* — WHAT I LIKED... WHAT I WOULD CHANGE...

☐ I PACKED WHAT I PLANNED ☐ I MADE SUBSTITUTIONS ☐ I DIDN'T MAKE A LUNCH

Grocery List

☐
☐
☐
☐
☐
☐
☐
☐
☐
☐
☐
☐
☐
☐
☐
☐
☐
☐
☐
☐
☐
☐
☐
☐

Leftovers /
groceries that
need to be used

✂

Date: _____   M T W Th F S Su

Recipes & Notes

DRINKS

SNACKS:

RATING ☆ ☆ ☆ ☆ ☆

Date: _____   M T W Th F S Su

Recipes & Notes

DRINKS

SNACKS:

RATING ☆ ☆ ☆ ☆ ☆

Date: _____   M T W Th F S Su

Recipes & Notes

DRINKS

SNACKS:

RATING ☆ ☆ ☆ ☆ ☆

Date: _____   M T W Th F S Su

Recipes & Notes

DRINKS

SNACKS:

RATING ☆ ☆ ☆ ☆ ☆

Prepare Ahead ——— WHAT I LIKED...　　WHAT I WOULD CHANGE... ———

□ I PACKED WHAT I PLANNED　　□ I MADE SUBSTITUTIONS　　□ I DIDN'T MAKE A LUNCH

Prepare Ahead ——— WHAT I LIKED...　　WHAT I WOULD CHANGE... ———

□ I PACKED WHAT I PLANNED　　□ I MADE SUBSTITUTIONS　　□ I DIDN'T MAKE A LUNCH

Prepare Ahead ——— WHAT I LIKED...　　WHAT I WOULD CHANGE... ———

□ I PACKED WHAT I PLANNED　　□ I MADE SUBSTITUTIONS　　□ I DIDN'T MAKE A LUNCH

Prepare Ahead ——— WHAT I LIKED...　　WHAT I WOULD CHANGE... ———

□ I PACKED WHAT I PLANNED　　□ I MADE SUBSTITUTIONS　　□ I DIDN'T MAKE A LUNCH

Grocery List

□
□
□
□
□
□
□
□
□
□
□
□
□
□
□
□
□
□
□
□
□
□
□
□

Leftovers /
groceries that
need to be used

✂

"A mother is a person who seeing there are only four pieces of pie for five people, promptly announces she never did care for pie." – Terneva Jordan

Date: _____ M T W Th F S Su

SNACKS:

DRINKS

Recipes & Notes

RATING ☆ ☆ ☆ ☆ ☆

Date: _____ M T W Th F S Su

SNACKS:

DRINKS

Recipes & Notes

RATING ☆ ☆ ☆ ☆ ☆

Date: _____ M T W Th F S Su

SNACKS:

DRINKS

Recipes & Notes

RATING ☆ ☆ ☆ ☆ ☆

Date: _____ M T W Th F S Su

SNACKS:

DRINKS

Recipes & Notes

RATING ☆ ☆ ☆ ☆ ☆

— *Prepare Ahead* ——— WHAT I LIKED...   WHAT I WOULD CHANGE...

☐ I PACKED WHAT I PLANNED   ☐ I MADE SUBSTITUTIONS   ☐ I DIDN'T MAKE A LUNCH

— *Prepare Ahead* ——— WHAT I LIKED...   WHAT I WOULD CHANGE...

☐ I PACKED WHAT I PLANNED   ☐ I MADE SUBSTITUTIONS   ☐ I DIDN'T MAKE A LUNCH

— *Prepare Ahead* ——— WHAT I LIKED...   WHAT I WOULD CHANGE...

☐ I PACKED WHAT I PLANNED   ☐ I MADE SUBSTITUTIONS   ☐ I DIDN'T MAKE A LUNCH

— *Prepare Ahead* ——— WHAT I LIKED...   WHAT I WOULD CHANGE...

☐ I PACKED WHAT I PLANNED   ☐ I MADE SUBSTITUTIONS   ☐ I DIDN'T MAKE A LUNCH

Grocery List

☐
☐
☐
☐
☐
☐
☐
☐
☐
☐
☐
☐
☐
☐
☐
☐
☐
☐
☐
☐
☐
☐
☐
☐

Leftovers /
groceries that
need to be used

"You waste life when you waste good food." – Katherine Anne Porter

Date: M T W Th F S Su

Recipes & Notes

DRINKS

SNACKS:

RATING ☆ ☆ ☆ ☆ ☆

Date: M T W Th F S Su

Recipes & Notes

DRINKS

SNACKS:

RATING ☆ ☆ ☆ ☆ ☆

Date: M T W Th F S Su

Recipes & Notes

DRINKS

SNACKS:

RATING ☆ ☆ ☆ ☆ ☆

Date: M T W Th F S Su

Recipes & Notes

DRINKS

SNACKS:

RATING ☆ ☆ ☆ ☆ ☆

— *Prepare Ahead* — WHAT I LIKED...   WHAT I WOULD CHANGE...

☐ I PACKED WHAT I PLANNED   ☐ I MADE SUBSTITUTIONS   ☐ I DIDN'T MAKE A LUNCH

— *Prepare Ahead* — WHAT I LIKED...   WHAT I WOULD CHANGE...

☐ I PACKED WHAT I PLANNED   ☐ I MADE SUBSTITUTIONS   ☐ I DIDN'T MAKE A LUNCH

— *Prepare Ahead* — WHAT I LIKED...   WHAT I WOULD CHANGE...

☐ I PACKED WHAT I PLANNED   ☐ I MADE SUBSTITUTIONS   ☐ I DIDN'T MAKE A LUNCH

— *Prepare Ahead* — WHAT I LIKED...   WHAT I WOULD CHANGE...

☐ I PACKED WHAT I PLANNED   ☐ I MADE SUBSTITUTIONS   ☐ I DIDN'T MAKE A LUNCH

Grocery List

☐
☐
☐
☐
☐
☐
☐
☐
☐
☐
☐
☐
☐
☐
☐
☐
☐
☐
☐
☐
☐
☐

Leftovers /
groceries that
need to be used

✂

"Cut my pie into four pieces, I don't think I could eat eight." – Yogi Berra

Date: _____ M T W Th F S Su

DRINKS

SNACKS:

RATING ☆ ☆ ☆ ☆ ☆

Recipes & Notes

Date: _____ M T W Th F S Su

DRINKS

SNACKS:

RATING ☆ ☆ ☆ ☆ ☆

Recipes & Notes

Date: _____ M T W Th F S Su

DRINKS

SNACKS:

RATING ☆ ☆ ☆ ☆ ☆

Recipes & Notes

Date: _____ M T W Th F S Su

DRINKS

SNACKS:

RATING ☆ ☆ ☆ ☆ ☆

Recipes & Notes

Prepare Ahead — WHAT I LIKED...   WHAT I WOULD CHANGE...

☐ I PACKED WHAT I PLANNED   ☐ I MADE SUBSTITUTIONS   ☐ I DIDN'T MAKE A LUNCH

Prepare Ahead — WHAT I LIKED...   WHAT I WOULD CHANGE...

☐ I PACKED WHAT I PLANNED   ☐ I MADE SUBSTITUTIONS   ☐ I DIDN'T MAKE A LUNCH

Prepare Ahead — WHAT I LIKED...   WHAT I WOULD CHANGE...

☐ I PACKED WHAT I PLANNED   ☐ I MADE SUBSTITUTIONS   ☐ I DIDN'T MAKE A LUNCH

Prepare Ahead — WHAT I LIKED...   WHAT I WOULD CHANGE...

Leftovers /
groceries that
need to be used

☐ I PACKED WHAT I PLANNED   ☐ I MADE SUBSTITUTIONS   ☐ I DIDN'T MAKE A LUNCH

☐
☐
☐
☐
☐
☐
☐
☐
☐
☐
☐
☐
☐
☐
☐
☐
☐
☐
☐
☐
☐
☐
☐

Date: _____ M T W Th F S Su

Recipes & Notes

DRINKS

SNACKS:

RATING ☆ ☆ ☆ ☆ ☆

Date: _____ M T W Th F S Su

Recipes & Notes

DRINKS

SNACKS:

RATING ☆ ☆ ☆ ☆ ☆

Date: _____ M T W Th F S Su

Recipes & Notes

DRINKS

SNACKS:

RATING ☆ ☆ ☆ ☆ ☆

Date: _____ M T W Th F S Su

Recipes & Notes

DRINKS

SNACKS:

RATING ☆ ☆ ☆ ☆ ☆

Prepare Ahead ———— WHAT I LIKED...   WHAT I WOULD CHANGE...

☐ I PACKED WHAT I PLANNED   ☐ I MADE SUBSTITUTIONS   ☐ I DIDN'T MAKE A LUNCH

Prepare Ahead ———— WHAT I LIKED...   WHAT I WOULD CHANGE...

☐ I PACKED WHAT I PLANNED   ☐ I MADE SUBSTITUTIONS   ☐ I DIDN'T MAKE A LUNCH

Prepare Ahead ———— WHAT I LIKED...   WHAT I WOULD CHANGE...

☐ I PACKED WHAT I PLANNED   ☐ I MADE SUBSTITUTIONS   ☐ I DIDN'T MAKE A LUNCH

Prepare Ahead ———— WHAT I LIKED...   WHAT I WOULD CHANGE...

☐ I PACKED WHAT I PLANNED   ☐ I MADE SUBSTITUTIONS   ☐ I DIDN'T MAKE A LUNCH

Grocery List

☐
☐
☐
☐
☐
☐
☐
☐
☐
☐
☐
☐
☐
☐
☐
☐
☐
☐
☐
☐
☐
☐

Leftovers /
groceries that
need to be used

"Appreciate the food your mother cooks for you. Some don't have food, others don't have mothers."

Date: M T W Th F S Su

DRINKS

SNACKS:

Recipes & Notes

RATING ☆ ☆ ☆ ☆ ☆

Date: M T W Th F S Su

DRINKS

SNACKS:

Recipes & Notes

RATING ☆ ☆ ☆ ☆ ☆

Date: M T W Th F S Su

DRINKS

SNACKS:

Recipes & Notes

RATING ☆ ☆ ☆ ☆ ☆

Date: M T W Th F S Su

DRINKS

SNACKS:

Recipes & Notes

RATING ☆ ☆ ☆ ☆ ☆

Prepare Ahead

WHAT I LIKED...   WHAT I WOULD CHANGE...

☐ I PACKED WHAT I PLANNED   ☐ I MADE SUBSTITUTIONS   ☐ I DIDN'T MAKE A LUNCH

Prepare Ahead

WHAT I LIKED...   WHAT I WOULD CHANGE...

☐ I PACKED WHAT I PLANNED   ☐ I MADE SUBSTITUTIONS   ☐ I DIDN'T MAKE A LUNCH

Prepare Ahead

WHAT I LIKED...   WHAT I WOULD CHANGE...

☐ I PACKED WHAT I PLANNED   ☐ I MADE SUBSTITUTIONS   ☐ I DIDN'T MAKE A LUNCH

Prepare Ahead

WHAT I LIKED...   WHAT I WOULD CHANGE...

☐ I PACKED WHAT I PLANNED   ☐ I MADE SUBSTITUTIONS   ☐ I DIDN'T MAKE A LUNCH

Grocery List

☐
☐
☐
☐
☐
☐
☐
☐
☐
☐
☐
☐
☐
☐
☐
☐
☐
☐
☐
☐
☐
☐
☐

Leftovers /
groceries that
need to be used

✂

"You don't have to do everything from scratch. Nobody wants to make puff pastry!"

– Ina Garten

Date: _____ M T W Th F S Su

Recipes & Notes

DRINKS

SNACKS: _____

RATING ☆ ☆ ☆ ☆ ☆

Date: _____ M T W Th F S Su

Recipes & Notes

DRINKS

SNACKS: _____

RATING ☆ ☆ ☆ ☆ ☆

Date: _____ M T W Th F S Su

Recipes & Notes

DRINKS

SNACKS: _____

RATING ☆ ☆ ☆ ☆ ☆

Date: _____ M T W Th F S Su

Recipes & Notes

DRINKS

SNACKS: _____

RATING ☆ ☆ ☆ ☆ ☆

— *Prepare Ahead* —————— WHAT I LIKED...   WHAT I WOULD CHANGE...

☐ I PACKED WHAT I PLANNED   ☐ I MADE SUBSTITUTIONS   ☐ I DIDN'T MAKE A LUNCH

— *Prepare Ahead* —————— WHAT I LIKED...   WHAT I WOULD CHANGE...

☐ I PACKED WHAT I PLANNED   ☐ I MADE SUBSTITUTIONS   ☐ I DIDN'T MAKE A LUNCH

— *Prepare Ahead* —————— WHAT I LIKED...   WHAT I WOULD CHANGE...

☐ I PACKED WHAT I PLANNED   ☐ I MADE SUBSTITUTIONS   ☐ I DIDN'T MAKE A LUNCH

— *Prepare Ahead* —————— WHAT I LIKED...   WHAT I WOULD CHANGE...

☐ I PACKED WHAT I PLANNED   ☐ I MADE SUBSTITUTIONS   ☐ I DIDN'T MAKE A LUNCH

Grocery List

☐
☐
☐
☐
☐
☐
☐
☐
☐
☐
☐
☐
☐
☐
☐
☐
☐
☐
☐
☐
☐
☐
☐

Leftovers /
groceries that
need to be used

✂

Date: _____ M T W Th F S Su

DRINKS

SNACKS:

Recipes & Notes

RATING ☆ ☆ ☆ ☆ ☆

Date: _____ M T W Th F S Su

DRINKS

SNACKS:

Recipes & Notes

RATING ☆ ☆ ☆ ☆ ☆

Date: _____ M T W Th F S Su

DRINKS

SNACKS:

Recipes & Notes

RATING ☆ ☆ ☆ ☆ ☆

Date: _____ M T W Th F S Su

DRINKS

SNACKS:

Recipes & Notes

RATING ☆ ☆ ☆ ☆ ☆

Prepare Ahead — WHAT I LIKED...   WHAT I WOULD CHANGE...

☐ I PACKED WHAT I PLANNED   ☐ I MADE SUBSTITUTIONS   ☐ I DIDN'T MAKE A LUNCH

Prepare Ahead — WHAT I LIKED...   WHAT I WOULD CHANGE...

☐ I PACKED WHAT I PLANNED   ☐ I MADE SUBSTITUTIONS   ☐ I DIDN'T MAKE A LUNCH

Prepare Ahead — WHAT I LIKED...   WHAT I WOULD CHANGE...

☐ I PACKED WHAT I PLANNED   ☐ I MADE SUBSTITUTIONS   ☐ I DIDN'T MAKE A LUNCH

Prepare Ahead — WHAT I LIKED...   WHAT I WOULD CHANGE...

☐ I PACKED WHAT I PLANNED   ☐ I MADE SUBSTITUTIONS   ☐ I DIDN'T MAKE A LUNCH

Grocery List

☐
☐
☐
☐
☐
☐
☐
☐
☐
☐
☐
☐
☐
☐
☐
☐
☐
☐
☐
☐
☐
☐
☐
☐

Leftovers /
groceries that
need to be used

✂

"There's one actual rule – the only rule in nutrition – and that is: Do what works for you!"
– Dr. Jade Teta

Date: _____ M T W Th F S Su

Recipes & Notes

DRINKS

SNACKS:

RATING ☆ ☆ ☆ ☆ ☆

Date: _____ M T W Th F S Su

Recipes & Notes

DRINKS

SNACKS:

RATING ☆ ☆ ☆ ☆ ☆

Date: _____ M T W Th F S Su

Recipes & Notes

DRINKS

SNACKS:

RATING ☆ ☆ ☆ ☆ ☆

Date: _____ M T W Th F S Su

Recipes & Notes

DRINKS

SNACKS:

RATING ☆ ☆ ☆ ☆ ☆

Prepare Ahead —————— WHAT I LIKED...   WHAT I WOULD CHANGE...

☐ I PACKED WHAT I PLANNED   ☐ I MADE SUBSTITUTIONS   ☐ I DIDN'T MAKE A LUNCH

Prepare Ahead —————— WHAT I LIKED...   WHAT I WOULD CHANGE...

☐ I PACKED WHAT I PLANNED   ☐ I MADE SUBSTITUTIONS   ☐ I DIDN'T MAKE A LUNCH

Prepare Ahead —————— WHAT I LIKED...   WHAT I WOULD CHANGE...

☐ I PACKED WHAT I PLANNED   ☐ I MADE SUBSTITUTIONS   ☐ I DIDN'T MAKE A LUNCH

Prepare Ahead —————— WHAT I LIKED...   WHAT I WOULD CHANGE...

☐ I PACKED WHAT I PLANNED   ☐ I MADE SUBSTITUTIONS   ☐ I DIDN'T MAKE A LUNCH

Grocery List

☐
☐
☐
☐
☐
☐
☐
☐
☐
☐
☐
☐
☐
☐
☐
☐
☐
☐
☐
☐
☐
☐
☐

Leftovers / groceries that need to be used

✂

"So what do I eat?', you ask…eat what mother nature so kindly provided us with! That's the good stuff!" – Dr. Andrew Saul

Date: _____ M T W Th F S Su

Recipes & Notes

DRINKS

SNACKS:

RATING ☆ ☆ ☆ ☆ ☆

Date: _____ M T W Th F S Su

Recipes & Notes

DRINKS

SNACKS:

RATING ☆ ☆ ☆ ☆ ☆

Date: _____ M T W Th F S Su

Recipes & Notes

DRINKS

SNACKS:

RATING ☆ ☆ ☆ ☆ ☆

Date: _____ M T W Th F S Su

Recipes & Notes

DRINKS

SNACKS:

RATING ☆ ☆ ☆ ☆ ☆

Prepare Ahead — WHAT I LIKED...   WHAT I WOULD CHANGE...

☐ I PACKED WHAT I PLANNED   ☐ I MADE SUBSTITUTIONS   ☐ I DIDN'T MAKE A LUNCH

Prepare Ahead — WHAT I LIKED...   WHAT I WOULD CHANGE...

☐ I PACKED WHAT I PLANNED   ☐ I MADE SUBSTITUTIONS   ☐ I DIDN'T MAKE A LUNCH

Prepare Ahead — WHAT I LIKED...   WHAT I WOULD CHANGE...

☐ I PACKED WHAT I PLANNED   ☐ I MADE SUBSTITUTIONS   ☐ I DIDN'T MAKE A LUNCH

Prepare Ahead — WHAT I LIKED...   WHAT I WOULD CHANGE...

☐ I PACKED WHAT I PLANNED   ☐ I MADE SUBSTITUTIONS   ☐ I DIDN'T MAKE A LUNCH

Grocery List

☐
☐
☐
☐
☐
☐
☐
☐
☐
☐
☐
☐
☐
☐
☐
☐
☐
☐
☐
☐
☐
☐
☐
☐

Leftovers /
groceries that
need to be used

✂

"Try organic food... or as your grandparents called it, FOOD."

Date: _____ M T W Th F S Su

Recipes & Notes

DRINKS

SNACKS: _____

RATING ☆ ☆ ☆ ☆ ☆

Date: _____ M T W Th F S Su

Recipes & Notes

DRINKS

SNACKS: _____

RATING ☆ ☆ ☆ ☆ ☆

Date: _____ M T W Th F S Su

Recipes & Notes

DRINKS

SNACKS: _____

RATING ☆ ☆ ☆ ☆ ☆

Date: _____ M T W Th F S Su

Recipes & Notes

DRINKS

SNACKS: _____

RATING ☆ ☆ ☆ ☆ ☆

Prepare Ahead — WHAT I LIKED...   WHAT I WOULD CHANGE...

☐ I PACKED WHAT I PLANNED   ☐ I MADE SUBSTITUTIONS   ☐ I DIDN'T MAKE A LUNCH

Prepare Ahead — WHAT I LIKED...   WHAT I WOULD CHANGE...

☐ I PACKED WHAT I PLANNED   ☐ I MADE SUBSTITUTIONS   ☐ I DIDN'T MAKE A LUNCH

Prepare Ahead — WHAT I LIKED...   WHAT I WOULD CHANGE...

☐ I PACKED WHAT I PLANNED   ☐ I MADE SUBSTITUTIONS   ☐ I DIDN'T MAKE A LUNCH

Prepare Ahead — WHAT I LIKED...   WHAT I WOULD CHANGE...

☐ I PACKED WHAT I PLANNED   ☐ I MADE SUBSTITUTIONS   ☐ I DIDN'T MAKE A LUNCH

☐
☐
☐
☐
☐
☐
☐
☐
☐
☐
☐
☐
☐
☐
☐
☐
☐
☐
☐
☐
☐
☐
☐

Leftovers / groceries that need to be used

✂

"Good food is very often, even most often, simple food."
– Anthony Bourdain

Date: _____ M T W Th F S Su ——— *Recipes & Notes* ———

DRINKS

SNACKS:

RATING ☆ ☆ ☆ ☆ ☆

Date: _____ M T W Th F S Su ——— *Recipes & Notes* ———

DRINKS

SNACKS:

RATING ☆ ☆ ☆ ☆ ☆

Date: _____ M T W Th F S Su ——— *Recipes & Notes* ———

DRINKS

SNACKS:

RATING ☆ ☆ ☆ ☆ ☆

Date: _____ M T W Th F S Su ——— *Recipes & Notes* ———

DRINKS

SNACKS:

RATING ☆ ☆ ☆ ☆ ☆

— *Prepare Ahead* — WHAT I LIKED... WHAT I WOULD CHANGE...

☐ I PACKED WHAT I PLANNED ☐ I MADE SUBSTITUTIONS ☐ I DIDN'T MAKE A LUNCH

— *Prepare Ahead* — WHAT I LIKED... WHAT I WOULD CHANGE...

☐ I PACKED WHAT I PLANNED ☐ I MADE SUBSTITUTIONS ☐ I DIDN'T MAKE A LUNCH

— *Prepare Ahead* — WHAT I LIKED... WHAT I WOULD CHANGE...

☐ I PACKED WHAT I PLANNED ☐ I MADE SUBSTITUTIONS ☐ I DIDN'T MAKE A LUNCH

— *Prepare Ahead* — WHAT I LIKED... WHAT I WOULD CHANGE...

☐ I PACKED WHAT I PLANNED ☐ I MADE SUBSTITUTIONS ☐ I DIDN'T MAKE A LUNCH

Grocery List

☐
☐
☐
☐
☐
☐
☐
☐
☐
☐
☐
☐
☐
☐
☐
☐
☐
☐
☐
☐
☐
☐
☐

Leftovers / groceries that need to be used

✂

191

*"If you go from 'I CAN'T have that' to
'I CAN have that but I don't want that' there is a massive paradigm shift!" – Jason Vale*

Date: _____ M T W Th F S Su

DRINKS

SNACKS:

Recipes & Notes

RATING ☆ ☆ ☆ ☆ ☆

Date: _____ M T W Th F S Su

DRINKS

SNACKS:

Recipes & Notes

RATING ☆ ☆ ☆ ☆ ☆

Date: _____ M T W Th F S Su

DRINKS

SNACKS:

Recipes & Notes

RATING ☆ ☆ ☆ ☆ ☆

Date: _____ M T W Th F S Su

DRINKS

SNACKS:

Recipes & Notes

RATING ☆ ☆ ☆ ☆ ☆

Prepare Ahead — WHAT I LIKED... WHAT I WOULD CHANGE...

☐ I PACKED WHAT I PLANNED   ☐ I MADE SUBSTITUTIONS   ☐ I DIDN'T MAKE A LUNCH

Prepare Ahead — WHAT I LIKED... WHAT I WOULD CHANGE...

☐ I PACKED WHAT I PLANNED   ☐ I MADE SUBSTITUTIONS   ☐ I DIDN'T MAKE A LUNCH

Prepare Ahead — WHAT I LIKED... WHAT I WOULD CHANGE...

☐ I PACKED WHAT I PLANNED   ☐ I MADE SUBSTITUTIONS   ☐ I DIDN'T MAKE A LUNCH

Prepare Ahead — WHAT I LIKED... WHAT I WOULD CHANGE...

☐ I PACKED WHAT I PLANNED   ☐ I MADE SUBSTITUTIONS   ☐ I DIDN'T MAKE A LUNCH

Grocery List

☐
☐
☐
☐
☐
☐
☐
☐
☐
☐
☐
☐
☐
☐
☐
☐
☐
☐
☐
☐
☐
☐

Leftovers / groceries that need to be used

✂

193

"Don't start a diet with an expiration date... Focus on a lifestyle that will last forever."

Date: _____ M T W Th F S Su

Recipes & Notes

DRINKS

SNACKS:

RATING ☆ ☆ ☆ ☆ ☆

Date: _____ M T W Th F S Su

Recipes & Notes

DRINKS

SNACKS:

RATING ☆ ☆ ☆ ☆ ☆

Date: _____ M T W Th F S Su

Recipes & Notes

DRINKS

SNACKS:

RATING ☆ ☆ ☆ ☆ ☆

Date: _____ M T W Th F S Su

Recipes & Notes

DRINKS

SNACKS:

RATING ☆ ☆ ☆ ☆ ☆

Prepare Ahead ——— WHAT I LIKED...   WHAT I WOULD CHANGE...

☐ I PACKED WHAT I PLANNED   ☐ I MADE SUBSTITUTIONS   ☐ I DIDN'T MAKE A LUNCH

Prepare Ahead ——— WHAT I LIKED...   WHAT I WOULD CHANGE...

☐ I PACKED WHAT I PLANNED   ☐ I MADE SUBSTITUTIONS   ☐ I DIDN'T MAKE A LUNCH

Prepare Ahead ——— WHAT I LIKED...   WHAT I WOULD CHANGE...

☐ ☐

☐ I PACKED WHAT I PLANNED   ☐ I MADE SUBSTITUTIONS   ☐ I DIDN'T MAKE A LUNCH

Prepare Ahead ——— WHAT I LIKED...   WHAT I WOULD CHANGE...

Leftovers /
groceries that
need to be used

☐ I PACKED WHAT I PLANNED   ☐ I MADE SUBSTITUTIONS   ☐ I DIDN'T MAKE A LUNCH

"Real food doesn't have ingredients. Real food is ingredients."

Date: _____ M T W Th F S Su

Recipes & Notes

DRINKS

SNACKS: _____

RATING ☆ ☆ ☆ ☆ ☆

Date: _____ M T W Th F S Su

Recipes & Notes

DRINKS

SNACKS: _____

RATING ☆ ☆ ☆ ☆ ☆

Date: _____ M T W Th F S Su

Recipes & Notes

DRINKS

SNACKS: _____

RATING ☆ ☆ ☆ ☆ ☆

Date: _____ M T W Th F S Su

Recipes & Notes

DRINKS

SNACKS: _____

RATING ☆ ☆ ☆ ☆ ☆

Prepare Ahead ——— WHAT I LIKED...   WHAT I WOULD CHANGE...

☐ I PACKED WHAT I PLANNED   ☐ I MADE SUBSTITUTIONS   ☐ I DIDN'T MAKE A LUNCH

Prepare Ahead ——— WHAT I LIKED...   WHAT I WOULD CHANGE...

☐ I PACKED WHAT I PLANNED   ☐ I MADE SUBSTITUTIONS   ☐ I DIDN'T MAKE A LUNCH

Prepare Ahead ——— WHAT I LIKED...   WHAT I WOULD CHANGE...

☐ I PACKED WHAT I PLANNED   ☐ I MADE SUBSTITUTIONS   ☐ I DIDN'T MAKE A LUNCH

Prepare Ahead ——— WHAT I LIKED...   WHAT I WOULD CHANGE...

☐ I PACKED WHAT I PLANNED   ☐ I MADE SUBSTITUTIONS   ☐ I DIDN'T MAKE A LUNCH

Grocery List

☐
☐
☐
☐
☐
☐
☐
☐
☐
☐
☐
☐
☐
☐
☐
☐
☐
☐
☐
☐
☐
☐
☐

Leftovers /
groceries that
need to be used

197

"What people don't realize is that food is not just calories: It's information. It actually contains messages that communicate to every cell in the body." – Dr. Mark Hyman

Date: _____ M T W Th F S Su

DRINKS

SNACKS:

RATING ☆ ☆ ☆ ☆ ☆

Recipes & Notes

Date: _____ M T W Th F S Su

DRINKS

SNACKS:

RATING ☆ ☆ ☆ ☆ ☆

Recipes & Notes

Date: _____ M T W Th F S Su

DRINKS

SNACKS:

RATING ☆ ☆ ☆ ☆ ☆

Recipes & Notes

Date: _____ M T W Th F S Su

DRINKS

SNACKS:

RATING ☆ ☆ ☆ ☆ ☆

Recipes & Notes

—— *Prepare Ahead* —— WHAT I LIKED...   WHAT I WOULD CHANGE...

☐ I PACKED WHAT I PLANNED   ☐ I MADE SUBSTITUTIONS   ☐ I DIDN'T MAKE A LUNCH

—— *Prepare Ahead* —— WHAT I LIKED...   WHAT I WOULD CHANGE...

☐
☐
☐
☐
☐
☐
☐
☐
☐
☐
☐
☐
☐
☐
☐
☐
☐
☐

☐ I PACKED WHAT I PLANNED   ☐ I MADE SUBSTITUTIONS   ☐ I DIDN'T MAKE A LUNCH

—— *Prepare Ahead* —— WHAT I LIKED...   WHAT I WOULD CHANGE...

☐
☐
☐
☐
☐
☐
☐
☐

☐ I PACKED WHAT I PLANNED   ☐ I MADE SUBSTITUTIONS   ☐ I DIDN'T MAKE A LUNCH

—— *Prepare Ahead* —— WHAT I LIKED...   WHAT I WOULD CHANGE...

Leftovers /
groceries that
need to be used

✂

☐ I PACKED WHAT I PLANNED   ☐ I MADE SUBSTITUTIONS   ☐ I DIDN'T MAKE A LUNCH

199

"Food is the best thing money can buy – Nothing else matters when you have an empty stomach."

Date: _____ M T W Th F S Su

Recipes & Notes

DRINKS

SNACKS: _____

RATING ☆ ☆ ☆ ☆ ☆

Date: _____ M T W Th F S Su

Recipes & Notes

DRINKS

SNACKS: _____

RATING ☆ ☆ ☆ ☆ ☆

Date: _____ M T W Th F S Su

Recipes & Notes

DRINKS

SNACKS: _____

RATING ☆ ☆ ☆ ☆ ☆

Date: _____ M T W Th F S Su

Recipes & Notes

DRINKS

SNACKS: _____

RATING ☆ ☆ ☆ ☆ ☆

— *Prepare Ahead* —   WHAT I LIKED...   WHAT I WOULD CHANGE...

☐
☐
☐
☐
☐
☐
☐
☐
☐
☐
☐
☐
☐
☐
☐

☐ I PACKED WHAT I PLANNED   ☐ I MADE SUBSTITUTIONS   ☐ I DIDN'T MAKE A LUNCH

— *Prepare Ahead* —   WHAT I LIKED...   WHAT I WOULD CHANGE...

☐
☐
☐
☐
☐
☐
☐
☐

☐ I PACKED WHAT I PLANNED   ☐ I MADE SUBSTITUTIONS   ☐ I DIDN'T MAKE A LUNCH

— *Prepare Ahead* —   WHAT I LIKED...   WHAT I WOULD CHANGE...

☐ I PACKED WHAT I PLANNED   ☐ I MADE SUBSTITUTIONS   ☐ I DIDN'T MAKE A LUNCH

— *Prepare Ahead* —   WHAT I LIKED...   WHAT I WOULD CHANGE...

Leftovers /
groceries that
need to be used

✂

☐ I PACKED WHAT I PLANNED   ☐ I MADE SUBSTITUTIONS   ☐ I DIDN'T MAKE A LUNCH

"Nourish your body as nature intended. Eat seasonally."

Date: _____ M T W Th F S Su

DRINKS

SNACKS:

Recipes & Notes

RATING ☆ ☆ ☆ ☆ ☆

Date: _____ M T W Th F S Su

DRINKS

SNACKS:

Recipes & Notes

RATING ☆ ☆ ☆ ☆ ☆

Date: _____ M T W Th F S Su

DRINKS

SNACKS:

Recipes & Notes

RATING ☆ ☆ ☆ ☆ ☆

Date: _____ M T W Th F S Su

DRINKS

SNACKS:

Recipes & Notes

RATING ☆ ☆ ☆ ☆ ☆

Prepare Ahead — WHAT I LIKED...   WHAT I WOULD CHANGE...

☐ I PACKED WHAT I PLANNED   ☐ I MADE SUBSTITUTIONS   ☐ I DIDN'T MAKE A LUNCH

Prepare Ahead — WHAT I LIKED...   WHAT I WOULD CHANGE...

☐ I PACKED WHAT I PLANNED   ☐ I MADE SUBSTITUTIONS   ☐ I DIDN'T MAKE A LUNCH

Prepare Ahead — WHAT I LIKED...   WHAT I WOULD CHANGE...

☐ I PACKED WHAT I PLANNED   ☐ I MADE SUBSTITUTIONS   ☐ I DIDN'T MAKE A LUNCH

Prepare Ahead — WHAT I LIKED...   WHAT I WOULD CHANGE...

☐ I PACKED WHAT I PLANNED   ☐ I MADE SUBSTITUTIONS   ☐ I DIDN'T MAKE A LUNCH

Grocery List

☐
☐
☐
☐
☐
☐
☐
☐
☐
☐
☐
☐
☐
☐
☐
☐
☐
☐
☐
☐
☐
☐
☐
☐

Leftovers /
groceries that
need to be used

✂

203

Date: M T W Th F S Su   *Recipes & Notes*

DRINKS

SNACKS:

RATING ☆ ☆ ☆ ☆ ☆

Date: M T W Th F S Su   *Recipes & Notes*

DRINKS

SNACKS:

RATING ☆ ☆ ☆ ☆ ☆

Date: M T W Th F S Su   *Recipes & Notes*

DRINKS

SNACKS:

RATING ☆ ☆ ☆ ☆ ☆

Date: M T W Th F S Su   *Recipes & Notes*

DRINKS

SNACKS:

RATING ☆ ☆ ☆ ☆ ☆

— *Prepare Ahead* — WHAT I LIKED... WHAT I WOULD CHANGE...

☐
☐
☐
☐
☐
☐
☐

☐ I PACKED WHAT I PLANNED   ☐ I MADE SUBSTITUTIONS   ☐ I DIDN'T MAKE A LUNCH

— *Prepare Ahead* — WHAT I LIKED... WHAT I WOULD CHANGE...

☐
☐
☐
☐
☐
☐

☐ I PACKED WHAT I PLANNED   ☐ I MADE SUBSTITUTIONS   ☐ I DIDN'T MAKE A LUNCH

— *Prepare Ahead* — WHAT I LIKED... WHAT I WOULD CHANGE...

☐
☐
☐
☐
☐
☐
☐

☐ I PACKED WHAT I PLANNED   ☐ I MADE SUBSTITUTIONS   ☐ I DIDN'T MAKE A LUNCH

— *Prepare Ahead* — WHAT I LIKED... WHAT I WOULD CHANGE...

Leftovers /
groceries that
need to be used

✂

☐ I PACKED WHAT I PLANNED   ☐ I MADE SUBSTITUTIONS   ☐ I DIDN'T MAKE A LUNCH

205

Date: _____ M T W Th F S Su

Recipes & Notes

DRINKS

_____
_____
_____
_____
_____
_____
_____
_____

SNACKS:

RATING ☆ ☆ ☆ ☆ ☆

Date: _____ M T W Th F S Su

Recipes & Notes

DRINKS

_____
_____
_____
_____
_____
_____
_____
_____

SNACKS:

RATING ☆ ☆ ☆ ☆ ☆

Date: _____ M T W Th F S Su

Recipes & Notes

DRINKS

_____
_____
_____
_____
_____
_____
_____
_____

SNACKS:

RATING ☆ ☆ ☆ ☆ ☆

Date: _____ M T W Th F S Su

Recipes & Notes

DRINKS

_____
_____
_____
_____
_____
_____
_____
_____

SNACKS:

RATING ☆ ☆ ☆ ☆ ☆

Prepare Ahead — WHAT I LIKED...   WHAT I WOULD CHANGE...

☐ I PACKED WHAT I PLANNED   ☐ I MADE SUBSTITUTIONS   ☐ I DIDN'T MAKE A LUNCH

Prepare Ahead — WHAT I LIKED...   WHAT I WOULD CHANGE...

☐ I PACKED WHAT I PLANNED   ☐ I MADE SUBSTITUTIONS   ☐ I DIDN'T MAKE A LUNCH

Prepare Ahead — WHAT I LIKED...   WHAT I WOULD CHANGE...

☐ I PACKED WHAT I PLANNED   ☐ I MADE SUBSTITUTIONS   ☐ I DIDN'T MAKE A LUNCH

Prepare Ahead — WHAT I LIKED...   WHAT I WOULD CHANGE...

☐ I PACKED WHAT I PLANNED   ☐ I MADE SUBSTITUTIONS   ☐ I DIDN'T MAKE A LUNCH

☐
☐
☐
☐
☐
☐
☐
☐
☐
☐
☐
☐
☐
☐
☐
☐
☐
☐
☐
☐
☐
☐
☐

Leftovers /
groceries that
need to be used

✂

207

"If I share my food with you, it's either because I love you a lot or because it fell on the floor and I don't want it."

Date: _____   M   T   W   Th   F   S   Su

Recipes & Notes

DRINKS

SNACKS:

RATING ☆ ☆ ☆ ☆ ☆

Date: _____   M   T   W   Th   F   S   Su

Recipes & Notes

DRINKS

SNACKS:

RATING ☆ ☆ ☆ ☆ ☆

Date: _____   M   T   W   Th   F   S   Su

Recipes & Notes

DRINKS

SNACKS:

RATING ☆ ☆ ☆ ☆ ☆

Date: _____   M   T   W   Th   F   S   Su

Recipes & Notes

DRINKS

SNACKS:

RATING ☆ ☆ ☆ ☆ ☆

— *Prepare Ahead* ———— WHAT I LIKED...   WHAT I WOULD CHANGE...

☐ I PACKED WHAT I PLANNED   ☐ I MADE SUBSTITUTIONS   ☐ I DIDN'T MAKE A LUNCH

— *Prepare Ahead* ———— WHAT I LIKED...   WHAT I WOULD CHANGE...

☐ I PACKED WHAT I PLANNED   ☐ I MADE SUBSTITUTIONS   ☐ I DIDN'T MAKE A LUNCH

— *Prepare Ahead* ———— WHAT I LIKED...   WHAT I WOULD CHANGE...

☐ I PACKED WHAT I PLANNED   ☐ I MADE SUBSTITUTIONS   ☐ I DIDN'T MAKE A LUNCH

— *Prepare Ahead* ———— WHAT I LIKED...   WHAT I WOULD CHANGE...

☐ I PACKED WHAT I PLANNED   ☐ I MADE SUBSTITUTIONS   ☐ I DIDN'T MAKE A LUNCH

Grocery List

☐
☐
☐
☐
☐
☐
☐
☐
☐
☐
☐
☐
☐
☐
☐
☐
☐
☐
☐
☐
☐
☐

Leftovers / groceries that need to be used

✂

Date: M T W Th F S Su   *Recipes & Notes*

DRINKS

SNACKS:

RATING ☆ ☆ ☆ ☆ ☆

Date: M T W Th F S Su   *Recipes & Notes*

DRINKS

SNACKS:

RATING ☆ ☆ ☆ ☆ ☆

Date: M T W Th F S Su   *Recipes & Notes*

DRINKS

SNACKS:

RATING ☆ ☆ ☆ ☆ ☆

Date: M T W Th F S Su   *Recipes & Notes*

DRINKS

SNACKS:

RATING ☆ ☆ ☆ ☆ ☆

— *Prepare Ahead* ——————— WHAT I LIKED...   WHAT I WOULD CHANGE...

☐ ☐

☐ I PACKED WHAT I PLANNED   ☐ I MADE SUBSTITUTIONS   ☐ I DIDN'T MAKE A LUNCH

— *Prepare Ahead* ——————— WHAT I LIKED...   WHAT I WOULD CHANGE...

☐ I PACKED WHAT I PLANNED   ☐ I MADE SUBSTITUTIONS   ☐ I DIDN'T MAKE A LUNCH

— *Prepare Ahead* ——————— WHAT I LIKED...   WHAT I WOULD CHANGE...

☐ I PACKED WHAT I PLANNED   ☐ I MADE SUBSTITUTIONS   ☐ I DIDN'T MAKE A LUNCH

— *Prepare Ahead* ——————— WHAT I LIKED...   WHAT I WOULD CHANGE...

Leftovers /
groceries that
need to be used

✂

☐ I PACKED WHAT I PLANNED   ☐ I MADE SUBSTITUTIONS   ☐ I DIDN'T MAKE A LUNCH

Date: M T W Th F S Su   *Recipes & Notes*

DRINKS

SNACKS:

RATING ☆ ☆ ☆ ☆ ☆

Date: M T W Th F S Su   *Recipes & Notes*

DRINKS

SNACKS:

RATING ☆ ☆ ☆ ☆ ☆

Date: M T W Th F S Su   *Recipes & Notes*

DRINKS

SNACKS:

RATING ☆ ☆ ☆ ☆ ☆

Date: M T W Th F S Su   *Recipes & Notes*

DRINKS

SNACKS:

RATING ☆ ☆ ☆ ☆ ☆

— *Prepare Ahead* ———— WHAT I LIKED...   WHAT I WOULD CHANGE...

☐ I PACKED WHAT I PLANNED   ☐ I MADE SUBSTITUTIONS   ☐ I DIDN'T MAKE A LUNCH

— *Prepare Ahead* ———— WHAT I LIKED...   WHAT I WOULD CHANGE...

☐ I PACKED WHAT I PLANNED   ☐ I MADE SUBSTITUTIONS   ☐ I DIDN'T MAKE A LUNCH

— *Prepare Ahead* ———— WHAT I LIKED...   WHAT I WOULD CHANGE...

☐ I PACKED WHAT I PLANNED   ☐ I MADE SUBSTITUTIONS   ☐ I DIDN'T MAKE A LUNCH

— *Prepare Ahead* ———— WHAT I LIKED...   WHAT I WOULD CHANGE...

☐ I PACKED WHAT I PLANNED   ☐ I MADE SUBSTITUTIONS   ☐ I DIDN'T MAKE A LUNCH

Grocery List

☐
☐
☐
☐
☐
☐
☐
☐
☐
☐
☐
☐
☐
☐
☐
☐
☐
☐
☐
☐
☐
☐

Leftovers /
groceries that
need to be used

✂

"HURRAY! – You made it through a FULL YEAR of packed LUNCHES!"

Date: _____ M T W Th F S Su

Recipes & Notes

DRINKS

SNACKS:

RATING ☆ ☆ ☆ ☆ ☆

Date: _____ M T W Th F S Su

Recipes & Notes

DRINKS

SNACKS:

RATING ☆ ☆ ☆ ☆ ☆

Date: _____ M T W Th F S Su

Recipes & Notes

DRINKS

SNACKS:

RATING ☆ ☆ ☆ ☆ ☆

Date: _____ M T W Th F S Su

Recipes & Notes

DRINKS

SNACKS:

RATING ☆ ☆ ☆ ☆ ☆

Prepare Ahead ——————————— WHAT I LIKED...   WHAT I WOULD CHANGE... ———————————

☐ I PACKED WHAT I PLANNED   ☐ I MADE SUBSTITUTIONS   ☐ I DIDN'T MAKE A LUNCH

Prepare Ahead ——————————— WHAT I LIKED...   WHAT I WOULD CHANGE... ———————————

☐ I PACKED WHAT I PLANNED   ☐ I MADE SUBSTITUTIONS   ☐ I DIDN'T MAKE A LUNCH

Prepare Ahead ——————————— WHAT I LIKED...   WHAT I WOULD CHANGE... ———————————

☐ I PACKED WHAT I PLANNED   ☐ I MADE SUBSTITUTIONS   ☐ I DIDN'T MAKE A LUNCH

Prepare Ahead ——————————— WHAT I LIKED...   WHAT I WOULD CHANGE... ———————————

☐ I PACKED WHAT I PLANNED   ☐ I MADE SUBSTITUTIONS   ☐ I DIDN'T MAKE A LUNCH

Grocery List

☐
☐
☐
☐
☐
☐
☐
☐
☐
☐
☐
☐
☐
☐
☐
☐
☐
☐
☐
☐
☐
☐
☐
☐
☐

Leftovers /
groceries that
need to be used

✂

215

Year in lunches

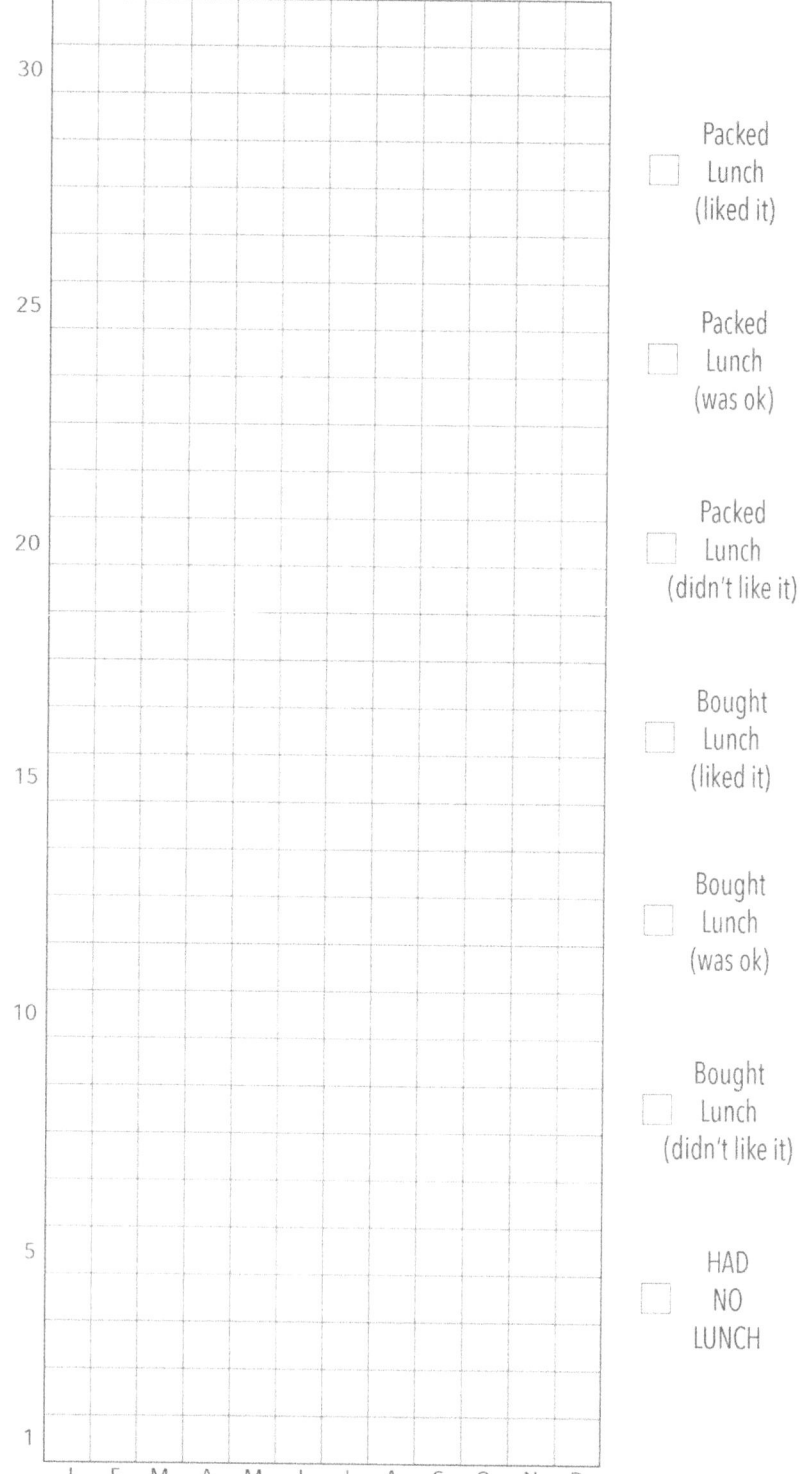

Packed Lunch (liked it)

Packed Lunch (was ok)

Packed Lunch (didn't like it)

Bought Lunch (liked it)

Bought Lunch (was ok)

Bought Lunch (didn't like it)

HAD NO LUNCH

30

25

20

15

10

5

1

J F M A M J J A S O N D

Weekly Lunch Planner

MONDAY

SNACKS: _____

TUESDAY

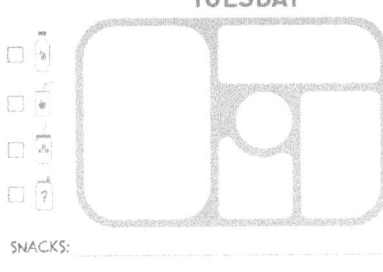

SNACKS: _____

WEDNESDAY

SNACKS: _____

THURSDAY

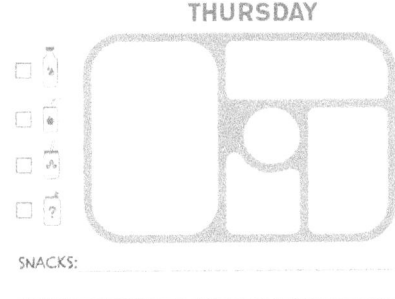

SNACKS: _____

FRIDAY

SNACKS: _____

SATURDAY

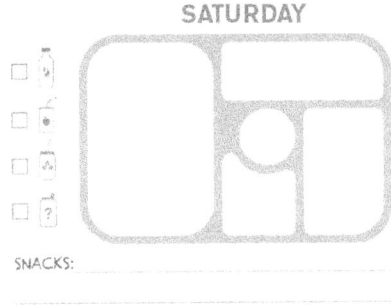

SNACKS: _____

SUNDAY

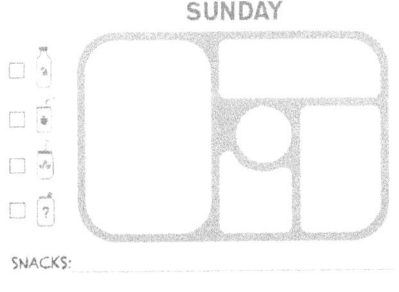

SNACKS: _____

EXTRA: _____

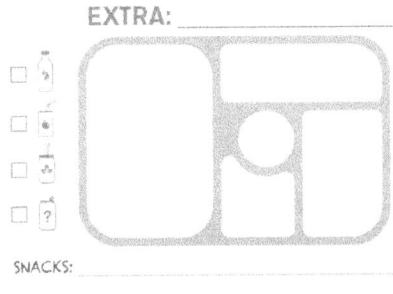

SNACKS: _____

Planning ahead...

CALENDAR YEAR

January

Sun	Mon	Tue	Wed	Thu	Fri	Sat

February

Sun	Mon	Tue	Wed	Thu	Fri	Sat

March

Sun	Mon	Tue	Wed	Thu	Fri	Sat

April

Sun	Mon	Tue	Wed	Thu	Fri	Sat

May

Sun	Mon	Tue	Wed	Thu	Fri	Sat

June

Sun	Mon	Tue	Wed	Thu	Fri	Sat

July

Sun	Mon	Tue	Wed	Thu	Fri	Sat

August

Sun	Mon	Tue	Wed	Thu	Fri	Sat

September

Sun	Mon	Tue	Wed	Thu	Fri	Sat

October

Sun	Mon	Tue	Wed	Thu	Fri	Sat

November

Sun	Mon	Tue	Wed	Thu	Fri	Sat

December

Sun	Mon	Tue	Wed	Thu	Fri	Sat

*Fill this out for the year and mark down the days where you will not need a lunch.

Don't forget to add...
Lunch Notes & Jokes

REUSABLE

REMINDER

This LUNCH
was made with
Love
xoxo

You're the **APPLE** *of my eye!*

YOU ARE BERRY
SPECIAL TO ME!

NOTE...

JOKE

WHY WAS 6 AFRAID OF 7?

Answer: Because 7 ate 9!

☆

YOU ARE AMAZING

A good angle to approach any problem is the TRY-angle!!

Never give up on what you Love

*Cut these out and laminate them or place them into card protectors to reuse!
>> Get more lunch notes & jokes from Lunchbox Love (www.sayplease.com)

227